DRUMMER BOY OF COMPANY C:
Coming of Age in the Civil War

DRUMMER BOY OF COMPANY C:
Coming of Age in the Civil War

Mary Louise Clifford

Cypress Communications
Alexandria, Virginia
2013

YB
Beneway, A

Design and layout by J. Candace Clifford. Printed in the USA by Global Printing, Alexandria, Virginia

Library of Congress Control Number: 2013938235

For more information:

www.CivilWarDrummerBoy.com
www.MaryLouiseClifford.com

Front cover image: Almon Beneway as Albert Walton from author's collection. The February 1863 muster roll for Company C of the Seventy-fifth Indiana Infantry Volunteers is in the background (National Archives Record Group 94). Albert's name is marked with an X. Back cover image is from Al's Compiled Military Service Record. Small illustrations on title page and below each chapter heading are based on Edwin Forbes's illustrations from the Morgan collection of Civil War drawings, Library of Congress LC-USZ62-79243 and LC-DIG-ppmsca-20586.

$ 19.95
5/22/14
SB

114006042

ACKNOWLEDGMENTS

Other individuals have provided invaluable assistance in filling out my grandfather's story. In a case of marvelous serendipity I found a first-cousin-once-removed on ancestry.com and discovered that she is the custodian of Almon's "memoir." Betty Beck generously brought the memoir to me and it became the foundation of Almon's story.

National Park Service Chief Historian Emeritus Edwin C. Bearss read the manuscript and wrote helpful comments in the margins. John C. Nelson drew the maps to my specifications and also read and commented on the first draft, as did Phyllis Hall Haislip and James Hart.

Years ago my father, Almon's son, Frank W. Beneway, at my request wrote down all he could remember of our family history, a document I have consulted many times in putting together Almon's story.

Members of the Military Reference Branch at the National Archives were most helpful in finding official documents: Juliette Arai, Jill D'Andrea, Trevor Plante, and Dennis Edelin. Military researchers Jonathan Deiss and Vonnie Zullo made valuable suggestions on tracking down obscure material.

Susannah Livingston is our dauntless copy editor.

CONTENTS

CHRONOLOGY

February 21, 1847	Almon was born.
April 12, 1861	Civil War began with shelling of Fort Sumter, South Carolina.
ca. July 1861	Al followed the Nineteenth Indiana Infantry Regiment to the Washington, D.C., area, became ill, and returned to Indianapolis.
ca. June 1862	Al ran away, changed his name, and joined the regimental band of the Sixtieth Indiana Infantry Volunteers.
August 19, 1862	Seventy-fifth Indiana Infantry Volunteer Regiment was mustered into service in Indianapolis.
August 21, 1862	Seventy-fifth Indiana moved to Louisville, Kentucky.
September 1, 1862	Almon was mustered into service in the Seventy-fifth Indiana Infantry as Albert Walton.
September 22, 1862	Emancipation Proclamation issued, to be effective January 1, 1863.
September - December 1862	Seventy-fifth pursued Confederate General Morgan's forces in Kentucky and Tennessee.
December 31, 1862	Battle of Stones River, Murfreesboro, Tennessee (Seventy-fifth arrived too late to participate).
January 1863	Seventy-fifth Indiana set up winter camp in Murfreesboro, Tennessee.
June 13, 1863	Tullahoma campaign began. Seventy-fifth Indiana left Murfreesboro.

June 24 - 26, 1863	Seventy-fifth skirmished at Hoover's Gap, Tennessee, pushing back Confederates.
June 30, 1863	Confederate General Bragg evacuated Tullahoma, Tennessee, retreating to Chattanooga.
July 1 - 4, 1863	Army of the Cumberland occupied Tullahoma.
July 3 - 5, 1863	Federal victories at Gettysburg, Pennsylvania, and Vicksburg, Mississippi.
August 21, 1863	Federal army shelled Chattanooga while Seventy-fifth marched to Chickamauga.
September 7 - 9, 1863	Confederates evacuated Chattanooga.
September 19 - 20, 1863	Battle of Chickamauga, Georgia; Al captured.
September 21 - 22, 1863	Federal army retreated to Chattanooga.
September 29, 1863	Federal prisoners, Al among them, sent to Richmond, Virginia.
December 12, 1863	Al transferred from Richmond to Danville, Virginia.
February 1864	Al transferred from Danville to Andersonville, Georgia.
October 1864	Al transferred from Andersonville to Florence, South Carolina.
November 30, 1864	Al paroled at Savannah, Georgia.
December 10, 1864	Al sent to Camp Parole, Maryland.
January 16, 1865	Al arrived at Camp Chase, Ohio.
April 22, 1865	Al rejoined his regiment at Holly Spring, North Carolina.
June 8, 1865	Seventy-fifth Indiana Infantry Volunteers mustered out of service.

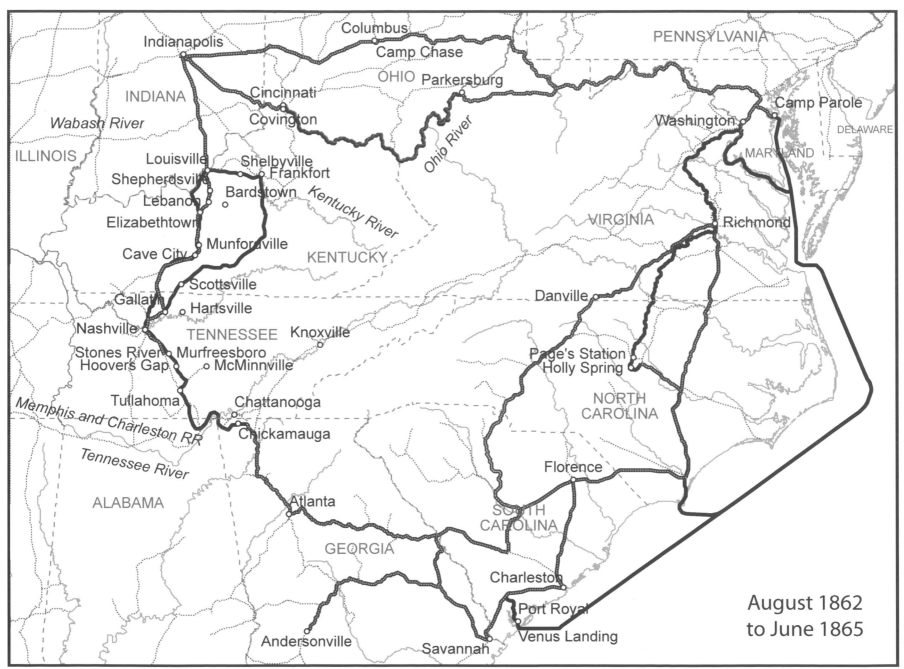

Columbus
Camp Chase
OHIO
Parkersburg
Indianapolis
INDIANA
Cincinnati
Covington
Wabash River
ILLINOIS
Louisville
Shelbyville
Shepherdsville
Frankfort
Bardstown
Lebanon
Kentucky River
Elizabethtown
Cave City
Munfordville
KENTUCKY
Scottsville
Gallatin
Hartsville
Nashville
TENNESSEE
Knoxville
Stones River
Murfreesboro
Hoover's Gap
McMinnville
Tullahoma
Chattanooga
Memphis and Charleston RR
Chickamauga
Tennessee River
ALABAMA
Atlanta
GEORGIA
Andersonville
Savannah

PENNSYLVANIA
Camp Parole
Washington
DELAWARE
MARYLAND
VIRGINIA
Richmond
Danville
Page's Station
Holly Spring
NORTH CAROLINA
Florence
SOUTH CAROLINA
Charleston
Port Royal
Venus Landing

August 1862
to June 1865

Broken lines indicate railroads. Solid lines show routes that were traveled either on foot or by ship. Maps by John C. Nelson <worldwidehistorymaps.com>.

FOREWORD

My grandfather was a drummer boy during the Civil War. You may wonder how that's possible when that war took place 150 years ago. Do the math. My father was born in 1884, when his father (the drummer boy) was 37. I was born in 1926, when my father was 42. My grandfather died the year I was born. It's easy to figure out how ancient I am now.

Are you wondering why I've waited so long?

The answer is simple: Some essential facts were missing. I've been gathering bits and pieces of information for more than 50 years. Some years ago, before computers were invented, I tried to find my grandfather on microfilm of the 1860 census, without success. I was looking in Fort Wayne, Indiana, based on what my father knew, but Almon wasn't in Fort Wayne in 1860. The National Archives now has the censuses online, so at the click of a mouse, I was able to find out where he was in both 1850 and 1860. I found a lot of other fascinating information online as well.

My initial interest was prompted by my father's retelling of his father's stories, but to that I can now add primary sources—most important of which is a 24-page, hand-written memoir (carefully preserved by a great-granddaughter) dictated by Almon himself in about 1920 to his daughters Myrtle and Grace. Other important sources include census records, the published history of Almon's regiment, a diary written by a member of his regiment, a memoir by another prisoner of war, Almon's obituary, military service records, pension applications, and various War Department records regarding Civil War prisoners and prisons.

> Primary sources are accounts by people who actually participated in an event, documents relating to that event, and official records of any kind that explain the event.

Clinton Hollow NY
March 1st 1904

Dear Sir
     the Battles of Chicamauga and Missionary
Ridge and the Challanoga Campaigner
played Sad havoc with our Company
I was taken Prisoner at Chickmauga
Sunday Evening Sept 20 ~~1863~~ 1863
Just at the close of the fight and held
for 14 months and ever Returned
to the Regiment While In the Carolinas
So you can See that much Could have
happened to Bortsfield In this
time that I would know nothing
about

          I am yours truly

          Albert Walton Beneway

There is a short letter from Almon, dated March 1, 1904, in the pension file of Private William H. Burchfield, alias William H. Bortsfield, Company C, Seventy-fifth Indiana Volunteers. The letter explains why Almon is unable to write an affidavit (a notarized statement) on Bortsfield's behalf. This letter is interesting because it shows that Almon had had enough schooling to write a coherent letter. School attendance was compulsory in the eastern and midwestern states, and some three-fifths of all children between the ages of five and 18 attended school on a regular basis.[1] In his signature here he has combined his alias, Albert Walton, with his real last name.

Almon and his family

CHAPTER 1   Almon and his family

Almon was born in 1847. Almon's father Egbert died in 1852. His mother Emily then married a man named Furman (or Freeman) Bacon in Poughkeepsie, New York. He took her to Harmony, Wisconsin, where he had a large family from an earlier marriage. Emily took her children Almon and Josephine there. Another son, named Robert Emile Bacon, was born while she lived with Mr. Bacon.

My father reported that Bacon was a cruel husband, and Emily left him. She appears in the 1860 census in Springfield, Illinois, along with five-year-old Emile, 13-year-old Almon, and 16-year-old Josephine, who is listed as Josephine White. The head of household is George White, a blacksmith, age 19. This indicates that Josephine may have married George White, or was at least living with him. No further information is available about George White.

Why Emily and her children were in Springfield is not clear either, unless they moved to Illinois to be near her former father-in-law James Beneway, who had settled briefly in DeKalb, Illinois. Nor is it clear how Almon came to be in Indianapolis in 1861 at the start of the Civil War.

Almon's memoir begins: "I resided at Indianapolis endeavoring to support my widowed[2] mother by selling newspapers on the street, before and after school. And as the reports of the firing on Fort Sumpter [*sic*] spread over the vast country, groups of men, filled with enthusiasm and love for their country, gathered on every corner, discussing many a serious question.

"They sought the newspapers and read everything that would give them any light on the affairs that were taking place all about them. They were patriotic men, their hearts burning with indignation and patriotism, and as the wild rumors reached their ears, they hysterically resolved that those country men who had fired on the dear old flag [at Fort Sumter] should be severely punished. In a few days Indiana commenced to equip her noble volunteers for the terrible struggle in view and send them out to battle for the right. The Nineteenth Regiment was one of the early regiments that enlisted at that time."

Clearly 14-year-old Almon was intrigued.

CHAPTER 1 ENDNOTES

[1] Don't be intimidated by endnotes. They supply important information without cluttering up the text. This information is from *Reluctant Witnesses* by Emily E. Werner, page 3. See bibliography for a complete citation.

[2] "Widowed" probably refers to Almon's dead father, not his stepfather.

Drawings of recruiting parties. Note the drummer boy. Harper's Weekly, *September 7, 1861, page 566.*

Almon and his family

CHAPTER 2   Almon runs away

The Civil War had begun. Recruiting parties, led by men who had already served in the war, came to major towns. With flags flying and drums beating, smartly uniformed officers beckoned to young men in the gathering crowd. Almon surely encountered such a spectacle. He watched the eager recruits signing the paper lying on the big drum. He noted that the drummer and the bugler were boys no older than himself. He listened to their stirring rhythms. He sensed them rousing the excitement of the onlookers. He thought, I could do that.

> Recruits are civilians whom the military seeks to enroll.

There was no minimum age for volunteers in the early part of the war.[1] Almon wrote in his memoir, "Much against the wishes of my Mother, I succeeded in entering Company D as a camp follower and being only a little past 14 years of age, they refused to muster me into service as a musician and being so anxious to take some part in the struggle for my country, I busied myself by brushing the lieutenant's uniform and blacking his shoes before he entered Dress Parade."

> To muster is to assemble. To be mustered in is to be enlisted and enrolled in military service. To be mustered out is to be discharged from military service.

When that same Nineteenth Regiment left Camp Morton for the front, Almon followed the regiment, which was sent to Virginia in August 1861 to bolster the Army of the Potomac. Somehow Almon acquired a uniform, much too big for him, and joined the swarm of cooks, mule drivers, wagon drivers and other camp followers that trailed every army in the field. They were fed, because they performed essential functions for the army. And occasionally they went out foraging in the countryside, lifting a chicken from a dooryard, finding a nest of eggs. Soldiers were not supposed to do this, but no one paid much attention to what a camp follower did. If Al brought fresh food into camp, he would have been welcomed by the enlisted men.

In his memoir, Almon wrote, "Our regiment was ordered to the front and on our arrival in Washington we were sent into camp at Kalorama Heights.[2] After a few weeks we changed camp and crossed the Chain Bridge, marched down through Georgetown to the Virginia side and here we labored diligently erecting fortifications. I often bathed in the swift current on the Potomac at Chain Bridge and took great delight in swimming. One day while enjoying myself in the water, I was seized by a cramp in my right arm and immediately lost my strength, and as I commenced to sink I screamed for help. A young man was standing on the rocks and upon hearing my shout, he sprang into the water and saved me from the angry billows. When we reached the shore I was so filled with joy that I offered him all the money I had, which was only five cents and my fishing line, but the kind fellow only laughed and thanked me.

"The regiment was ordered to Lewinsville crossroads where the rebels had two pieces of artillery, and as we approached the shells flew thick and fast, but we were successful in routing them out and returned to camp in triumph." This occurred in September 1861, when the 19th Regiment fought a small skirmish in Lewinsville, another at Falls Church, and then went into winter quarters at Fort Craig.

"As we lay in camp, I was taken sick with typhoid fever and taken to the Office Hospital; while there I was under the tender loving care of the Sisters of Mercy. In a short time I was able to walk about and one day while walking I met a gentleman who was visiting the hospital and soon were deeply engaged in conversation. He asked me to go home with him, telling me that his own son was dead and that he had come to take his body home. I consented and we were soon on our way home, while his own darling boy's body was in the baggage car ahead. I got off in Indianapolis while he journeyed on to Chicago, and I have never heard of him since."

"There were regiments at Camp Morton getting ready for the front, and I wanted to join them. My Mother had forbidden me going, but nothing would satisfy me. I was determined to be a drummer boy and finally succeeded in being mustered

Almon runs away

Band of the Eighth New York State Militia, June 1861. The cymbal player is in the back row, second from the left. Civil War Photograph Collection, Library of Congress, LC-DIG-ppmsc-02779.

into the band of the 60th Indiana Volunteers. My Mother would not consent to my going and came to camp and took me home, but when the boys were ready to start, I ran away." To elude his mother, he changed his name to Albert Walton.

In June 1862 the Sixtieth Indiana left the state for Louisville, Kentucky. "I received $12 a month and was given the position of cymbal player. We journeyed through Kentucky until we reached Lebanon Junction and here our Company D was to guard the junction while the remainder of the regiment was ordered to Munfordville, Kentucky, to meet Morgan, who was then parading through Kentucky, but they were obliged to surrender.

"Company D then received orders to return to Indianapolis, and when prepared, we marched from Lebanon Junction to Louisville. I did not want to go any further toward home, being afraid that my Mother would not let me go again. As we approached Louisville, I left my company and walked over to see the boys of the Seventy-fifth Indiana Infantry Volunteers."

Almon doesn't mention it, but in 1862 the War Department ended support for regimental bands, another reason that he would need to attach himself to some other army unit.

Some three million Americans served in the military during the four years of the Civil War. Al would eventually find his place in the Seventy-fifth Indiana Infantry Volunteers. According to the *History of the Seventy-fifth Regiment of Indiana Infantry Volunteers*,[4] the 10 companies composing that regiment were raised in the Eleventh Congressional District of Indiana. The camp of rendezvous was at Wabash, on the south bank of the Wabash River—four or five acres of timbered ground on the side of a hill. On August 18 the volunteers left Wabash by rail for Indianapolis.

I have difficulty thinking of him as Albert, but he probably chose the name because the nickname for both Almon and Albert is Al. So let's call him Al.

At the beginning of the war, brass bands were considered essential to every regiment. In June 1862, 14,000 bandsmen were serving in 618 bands. Due to the high cost of these bands—thousands of dollars—the War Department in July 1862 ordered all volunteer bands to be discontinued.

The "total amount of the articles of clothing and equipage … manufactured, purchased, etc., at the several depots of the quartermaster's department during the fiscal year ending June 30, 1864" included "9,018 bugles, 7,066 trumpets, 13,451 drums, and 14,830 fifes."[3]

Infantry are foot soldiers. Cavalry are soldiers mounted on horses. Artillery are the big guns, too heavy to carry, drawn by horses, manned by crews. Supplies in the army are provided by the quartermaster corps.

Rendezvous: A French term for a meeting place.

Almon runs away

HISTORY

OF THE

SEVENTY-FIFTH REGIMENT

OF

INDIANA INFANTRY VOLUNTEERS,

ITS

ORGANIZATION CAMPAIGNS, AND BATTLES.
(1862–65.)

BY
REV. DAVID BITTLE FLOYD, A. M.,
(FORMERLY A SERGEANT IN CO. *N* OF THE REGIMENT.)

WITH AN INTRODUCTION
BY
MAJOR-GENERAL J. J. REYNOLDS,
(PROVISIONAL COLONEL OF THE REGIMENT.)

———

PUBLISHED FOR THE AUTHOR.

———

PHILADELPHIA:
LUTHERAN PUBLICATION SOCIETY.
1893.

The History of the Seventy-fifth Regiment of Indiana Infantry Volunteers *was written by a member of the regiment, David Bittle Floyd, in a chatty way, from a first-person point of view. In quotations from the History that follow, "we" has been changed to "they" to conform with the third-person point of view of the rest of our story. Footnote citations will say simply* History.

SERGEANT DAVID B. FLOYD,
Author of this History, in his 17th year; born March 15th, 1846.

Sergeant David Bittle Floyd, who wrote the history of the Seventy-fifth Indiana Infantry Volunteers. This illustration is based on a photograph. As regiments were raised, local photographers enjoyed a brisk trade taking pictures of the new-fledged soldiers of the regiment dressed in their military accouterments and arms. History of the Seventy-fifth Regiment Indiana Infantry Volunteers, *page 20.*

On August 19, 1862, the regiment—a thousand men all told—was mustered into service in Indianapolis under the command of Colonel John U. Petit. Each of the 10 companies—A through K—had around 100 men. Officers of each company—one captain, two or three lieutenants, four sergeants and four corporals—were elected from among its recruits by the company casting ballots. Because they were known to each other, little formality existed between these raw farm boys and the men they chose to lead them. In fact, they didn't hesitate to talk back to them.

When Captain Francis M. Bryant told Company C that they were headed south, someone asked why. The Captain probably responded, "That's what the colonel ordered."

"Who tells the colonel?"

"The generals."

"Where are the generals?"

"In Washington."

"How do the generals tell the colonel?"

"Telegraph." That would have ended the discussion. How these things worked was not something they needed to worry about.

Each soldier was issued an ill-fitting uniform coat that reached to his ankles, one blanket, an oilcloth poncho, a water canteen, and a knapsack that would hold 30 to 50 pounds of surplus baggage—extra clothing, blankets, family keepsakes, and personal treasures. Each soldier had a tin plate, tin cup, a knife, fork, and spoon, and a haversack.

On the same evening of the muster, the soldiers formed a line and marched to the state arsenal. As each enlisted man presented

The regimental *History* offers a vivid description of the departure from Wabash:

"The bustle of preparation was mingled with the farewell of loved ones. Long before the hour of departure . . . men sang patriotic songs of joyfulness. About seven o'clock the Regiment marched to the depot, where box-cars were waiting to convey them to the place of muster.

"An immense crowd gathered to see them off. When they were 'all aboard,' passing out of the depot, they were greeted with shouts of good cheer by the assembled citizens.

"The eagerness on the part of the citizens along the route 'to greet and welcome the boys' who were on their way to war, was unprecedented. At every home—however humble—the windows and housetops were decorated with the flag of the nation. Relatives, friends, and acquaintances laid aside the duties of the day and resorted to the towns and depots along the way. They were determined to give the defenders of their homes and firesides a good send-off. . . . Men, women, and children by the thousand congregated at Kokomo, Tipton, and Noblesville with baskets of provisions, with which they fed the soldiers. In some instances, mementos were presented to the men, who carried them to the Southern camps and battle-fields, and a few of these mementos found their way into Southern prisons."[6]

Canteens were turned to many uses besides carrying water. They were constructed of two rounded pans welded together with a spout at one end. Broken apart, the two pans could be used to cook food over a fire, to carry food from a mess, to dig holes and tunnels, etc.

A haversack was a tarred cloth bag suspended by a shoulder strap in which a soldier carried his food rations.

Almon runs away

himself at a small window of the arsenal, he received a Springfield rifle and a cartridge box.

Because by late August two Confederate armies were moving north, threatening the cities of Covington and Louisville, Kentucky, and Cincinnati, Ohio, all the new regiments raised in the northwest were sent south to Kentucky, the Seventy-fifth among them. Their ultimate objective, which was to take control of the Memphis and Charleston railroad

The Springfield rifle is a muzzle-loading .58-caliber U.S. Army rifle-musket, first made in Springfield, Massachusetts.

The leather cartridge box was normally suspended from a shoulder sling and contained tin dividers holding 40 rounds of paper cartridge ammunition.

A company of Indiana infantry soldiers poses for the camera. Mathew Brady Photographs of Civil War-Era Personalities and Scenes, National Archives 111-B-289.

Drummer Boy of Company C

line between Nashville and Chattanooga, Tennessee (the only section they did not yet control), was probably never explained to the foot soldiers. This important railroad line gave the Confederates a direct connection between the Mississippi Valley region and the Atlantic seaboard.

On August 21 the Seventy-fifth Indiana Infantry Volunteers Regiment—1,036 strong—boarded the railroad cars at Indianapolis for Louisville, Kentucky. They slept rolled in their blankets, lying in rows.

"The journey was uneventful, except the ovations received from the citizens of the towns and villages through which they passed during the early part of the night. As they journeyed, women and children, through gratitude for the services expected from them, fed them on pies and cakes. They reached Louisville on the 23d, crossing the Ohio River at Jeffersonville about six o'clock in the morning, and marched to Camp Oakland, just outside the southern limits of the city. The regiment appeared, on the evening of the day of arrival, for Dress Parade[7] for the first time."[8]

After the arrival of Major General Don Carlos Buell's army at Louisville, the Seventy-fifth Regiment was one of three regiments making up the Twelfth Division, assigned to the Army of the Ohio under General Buell.

Confederate General Braxton Bragg's supply base was at Chattanooga and and General Kirby Smith's at Knoxville, Tennessee, with their Confederate armies heading for the Ohio River and reclaiming Kentucky as they went. From Louisville the Seventy-fifth Indiana Infantry Volunteers Regiment moved out of camp and formed its first Line of Battle with the expectation of an attack. They drilled often, performed daily guard and picket duty, and were startled when they saw enemy pickets.

"They were not really armies, although that is what men called them. They were just collections of very young men, most of whom knew nothing at all about the grim profession they had engaged in, all of them calling themselves soldiers but ignorant of what the word really meant. Day after tomorrow they would be soldiers, but now they were civilians, gawky in their new uniforms, each one dreaming that battle would be splendid and exciting, and that he himself would survive; and they came from North and South, from farm and cane-brake cabin and from small town and busy city, trudging the dusty roads and tensing themselves for the great test of manhood that seemed to lie just ahead."[5]

The Dress Parade was a test of military efficiency and a thorough drill; it was the finest demonstration of the accuracy of tactical training and the unity of a military organization.

Almon runs away

When Bragg's Confederate army advanced, the Seventy-fifth returned to Louisville. Al was already there, waiting, watching for another opportunity to enlist. In fact, the *History* says, "While at Louisville, a little blue-eyed, brown-haired and beardless boy came to our Regiment. He was dressed in the uniform of a soldier. He gave a vivid account of two unsuccessful attempts to become a drummer boy of a Regiment."[10]

In his memoir Al wrote that he "entered into conversation with them [the Seventy-fifth Indiana Infantry Volunteers] and what a jolly crew they were. I soon found myself conversing with the captain [Francis M. Bryant] and two sergeants. The captain asked me if I could drum and I remarked that I could. Then a drum was given to me and placing it against the tongue of a wagon, I played as if filled with a

An infantry company On Parade. Note the drummers at the left and the flag bearer in the center. Mathew Brady Photographs of Civil War-Era Personalities and Scenes, National Archives 111-B-284.

Because the battlegrounds of the Civil War stretched from the Atlantic Ocean to the Mississippi River, each campaign was conducted by a field army under a general. These field armies had names—thus the Army of the Potomac, the Army of the Ohio, the Army of the Cumberland, etc. Each was followed by vast numbers of white-covered wagons carrying food, forage for the horses and mules, and ammunition.

- A field army consisted of from two to five corps.
- A corps consisted of from two to five divisions.
- A division consisted of three brigades or regiments (1,500 to 5,000 soldiers).
- A brigade consisted of three or more regiments (1,000 to 1,500 soldiers).
- A regiment consisted of from two to three battalions.
- A battalion consisted of three to five companies (500 to 600 soldiers).
- A company consisted of two platoons (80 to 100 soldiers).
- A platoon consisted to three to four squads (20 to 40 soldiers).
- A squad had four to 10 soldiers.[9]

An infantry regiment moving out on Dress Parade. Mathew Brady Photographs of Civil War-Era Personalities and Scenes, National Archives 111-B-305.

Almon runs away

new spirit. A crowd soon gathered around me and I noticed the two sergeants talking earnestly with the captain.

"When I had finished playing, the captain came up and seizing my hand said, 'You will do, my son. I want you as my drummer for our company has none.' My heart swelled with joy and pride. Had I at last accomplished my desire, the one thing I had longed for so long?

"When my descriptive list was taken, I was four feet, seven inches high and fifteen years old. I was given a uniform which was much too large for me and as we marched down the street, the boys would holler, 'Coat, where are you going with the little man?' Little did we think during those merry days spent at Louisville what we were yet to undergo for the dear old flag.

"I was then placed in care of Sergeants [Arland O. D.] Kelly and [Jacob] Lair, and here was the commencement of a true friendship that was as deep as the ocean and as wide as its beds. I told the company of my misfortunes and they were greatly in sympathy with me. I was the child of the company and they were like brothers to me, giving me advice, petting me and looking after me."

Almon was mustered into the service on September 1, 1862, under the name of Albert Walton, as the musician of Company C of the Seventy-fifth Indiana Regiment.

Part of Al's Compiled Military Service Record. As did many soldiers, Al lied about his age. He was actually born near Poughkeepsie, but he may have claimed to be from New York City to help him evade his mother. National Archives.

W | 75 | **Ind.**

Albert Walton,

............, Co. C, 75 Reg't Indiana Infantry.

Appears on

Company Descriptive Book

of the organization named above.

DESCRIPTION.

Age 16 years; height 5 feet — inches.

Complexion *Light*

Eyes *Blue*; hair *Light*

Where born *City New York*

Occupation *Pedler.*

ENLISTMENT.

When *Sept. 1*, 1862.

Where *Louisville, Ky.*

By whom *R. M. Bryant*; term 3 y'rs.

Remarks: *Taken prisoner at the battle of Chickamauga Sept. 20 /63.*

Huxley

(383g)   Copyist

Two Civil War drummer boys became famous. Johnny Clem became a Union poster boy after his drum was smashed by artillery at Shiloh in 1862. He made a career of the army and retired in 1916 as a Quartermaster General, the last Civil War combatant on active duty. Little Red Cap (Ransom Powell), of a West Virginia scouting company, was captured and imprisoned at Andersonville, but the Confederate officials there took him out of the stockade and used him as an orderly, feeding and clothing him throughout. His *Memoirs of Little Red Cap,* written after the war, was published privately by Harold L. Scott in 1997.

A paragraph in the Seventy-fifth Indiana Volunteers regimental history about another drummer summarizes what was expected of these intrepid boys:

> The youngest member [of the Seventy-fifth] was Andrew H. Burke, the drummer of D Company. At the time of his enrollment he was a lad 12 years old, with wavy auburn hair and grayish-blue eyes. On account of his age he too had difficulty in obtaining muster into the service, but the mustering officer, General Carrington, admitted him into the Regiment. 'Andy' was the musician who, on an eventful Sunday morning before daylight at Lebanon, Kentucky, beat the long roll on his drum, which called the Regiment into the first line of battle. He was with them, carrying his drum at the head of the Regiment, through all the marches and raids in Kentucky and Tennessee, until they reached the town of Castalian Springs. Here, in December, he was taken sick with a scrofulous affection [*sic*],[11] on account of which, on January 5th, 1863, he was discharged. This drummer boy in 1862 is the governor of North Dakota in 1892.[12]

A third drummer boy, Henry Martyn Kieffer of the One Hundred Fifteenth Regiment, Pennsylvania Volunteers, wrote his recollections long after the Civil War in a series of vivid stories. They were published in 1889. A reproduction has recently been issued by the Library of Congress.

CHAPTER 2 ENDNOTES

[1] In 1864, Congress set a minimum age of 16 for enlistment.

[2] Kalorama Heights was a 30-acre parcel of land in north central Washington (now northwest of Dupont Circle) where a mansion was built by Joel Barlow after 1807. During the Civil War it was used as a smallpox hospital.

[3] From the "Annual Report of the Secretary of War to the Second Session of the Thirty-Eighth Congress," Ex. Doc. 83 (Washington, D.C.: Government Printing Office, 1865).

[4] Floyd, David Bittle, *History of the Seventy-fifth Regiment of Indiana Infantry Volunteers* (Philadelphia: Lutheran Publication Society, 1893). Henceforth referred to as "*History.*"

[5] Bruce Catton, *This Hallowed Ground* (New York: Doubleday & Company, 1956), p. 109.

[6] *History*, pp. 18-19.

[7] The names of drum rolls are capitalized throughout.

[8] *History*, p. 22.

[9] Found on U.S. Army website <www.army.mil/info/organization/unitsandcommands/oud/>. Revised in review by Edwin C. Bearss, March 16, 2013.

[10] *History*, p. 22.

[11] [*sic*] means the word is spelled wrong but this is how the writer spelled it.

[12] *History*, p. 24.

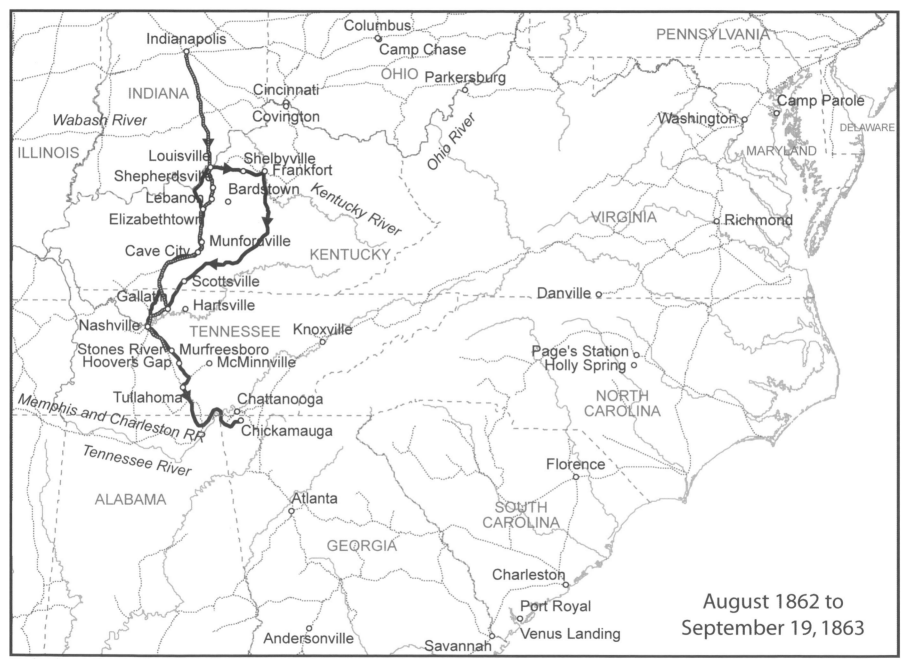

Broken lines indicate railroads. Solid lines show routes that were traveled either on foot or by ship. Lines without arrows indicate routes that Al traveled in both directions.

Camp life

CHAPTER 3   Camp life

The soldiers pitched their canvas tents along the roadside on the south side of Louisville, Kentucky, near Hardin Creek in an orderly, geometric layout of parallel company streets. Much of the regiment was quartered in square A tents holding six or seven men lined up close together to sleep. Al's C Company had conical Sibley tents resembling Indian tipis, in which two dozen men slept in a circular pattern around a stove with a pipe that exited through a hole at the apex of the tent.

The men carried rations in their haversacks and made fires to boil coffee and cook food. They ground up the coffee beans in tin pails using their musket butts. The hardtack could be softened by dipping it in their coffee.

When they marched, the men carried their knapsacks and blanket rolls, but the tents, as well as other equipment, food, and forage for the mules and horses, were piled in wooden wagons pulled by mules. After a few miles on the road, knapsacks became heavier and heavier, and keepsakes brought from home—books, embroidered pillows, quilts, pen cases—were often cast aside to lighten the load. When their wagon trains got stuck on muddy roads, the soldiers often had to bivouac without tents or rations. Horses and mules went hungry as well.

The color bearers carried both the Stars and Stripes and the regimental battle flag at the head of each day's march. The drummers and buglers led each company as they set out. The soldiers followed eagerly, their steps springy, their imaginations bright with visions of heroic victories ahead of them. Al was so excited he had difficulty slowing his drumbeat to a reasonable pace.

Field rations consisted of coffee beans, bread known as hardtack because of its rocklike consistency, and salted meat.

Hardtack was a square flour-and-water biscuit that could be improved by soaking in water and frying in sizzling fat. Often the hardtack was infested with weevils, which could be picked out or floated out in a cup of boiling coffee. The hardtack could also be ground into flour for making griddle cakes. Three chunks of hardtack were considered a meal, nine a daily ration.

The meat, usually pork, was preserved uncooked in barrels of brine strong enough to preserve the meat for two years. Regulations specified a daily issue of 20 ounces of salt beef or 12 ounces of salt pork.

Bivouac: A temporary encampment, or to camp out for the night.

A commissary tent with fresh beef hanging inside. The barrels and crates contain other provisions. Mathew Brady Photographs of Civil War-Era Personalities and Scenes, National Archives 111-B-249.

A wagon train waiting for supplies to be unloaded from river boats. Mathew Brady Photographs of Civil War-Era Personalities and Scenes, National Archives 111-B-5230.

Camp life

One of the three regimental color bearers belonged to Company C: Sergeant Jacob Lair, 22 years old, 5 feet 9 inches tall, dark complexion, brown eyes, black hair, a cooper before the war. While he and Al marched together at the head of their company, Sergeant Lair paid special attention to the much younger boy, joking with him as they strode along. Al soon admired Jacob and treasured his attention.

A color bearer has pitched his flag beside his tent. Mathew Brady Photographs of Civil War-Era Personalities and Scenes, National Archives 111-B-5429.

Brigadier General Ebenezer Dumont, Commander of the Twelfth Division. History of the Seventy-fifth Indiana Infantry Volunteers, *page 25.*

The Seventy-fifth Indiana camped by Hardin Creek until September 6, 1862. Al had long since gotten over being homesick, but he saw the first signs of it in his untested comrades who were still in their teens. To distract them, General Ebenezer Dumont, commander of the Twelfth Division, delivered an address to the regiment immediately on their arrival, in which he warned of the imminent possibility of an attack by Confederate General John Hunt Morgan's cavalry.[1] The threat diverted their attention from their own anxieties.

This was their time for learning the ropes. A regiment that had regular army officers was lucky because the officers knew camp routine. Volunteer officers had just as much to learn as the enlisted men. They all had to master company and regiment and brigade and division drill. Infantrymen had to learn guard, picket, and skirmish duty—basic skills for going into battle.

"In July 1862 Confederate cavalry under Brigadier John H. Morgan had burned Union commissary stores at Lebanon, and had committed other depredations in the vicinity. By October 1862 Morgan's cavalry was operating south of Louisville, threatening Bardstown, Elizabethtown, Shepherdsville, Louisville and Lebanon Junction.

"The Twelfth Division, just organized out of some of the new regiments of which the Seventy-fifth Indiana was one, was to occupy and defend these towns until the arrival of [General] Buell's army. The Division was placed under the command of Brigadier General Ebenezer Dumont, who had already gone to Lebanon with part of the Division."[2]

Pickets were sent out ahead of the regiment to watch for the appearance of the enemy. A skirmisher was a soldier sent ahead of the main body of troops to scout out and probe the enemy's position.

Camp life

An infantry camp. In the foreground is a mud-spattered forge. Beyond it, some mules are picketed around the wagons. Next you see a guard, their muskets stacked and knapsacks lying on the ground. Past them a cook sits on a mess chest close to the ashes of his fire. A regiment of infantry is drawn up in front of the camp tents, probably on an Inspection Drill. "Photographic Sketchbook of the Civil War" by Alexander Gardner, National Archives 165-SB-16.

Corporal William Bluffton Miller[3] of Company K in the Seventy-fifth Indiana Regiment kept a diary that provides an excellent description of picket duty: "Picket duty is done by dividing the men into three parties called 'reliefs' and a corporal to take charge of each. Then the 1st Relief is scattered along the line of stations so many paces apart. Generally about thirty and they are required to walk back and forth during the two hours they are on duty. They are relieved every two hours out of Six or 'two on and four off' as is known in the Army. The two reliefs not on duty are Stationed in the rear where guns are Stacked and ready for action if an attack is made on the Posts. They are Called Reserves. In case of an attack the pickets 'rally on the Reserve' and fall back toward camp untill [sic] a Line of Battle is formed to meet the attacking party."[4]

An infantry company at Parade Rest. Mathew Brady Photographs of Civil War-Era Personalities and Scenes, National Archives 111-B-280.

In the 12 days the Seventy-fifth spent by Hardin Creek, the soldiers were busy drilling, cleaning their rifles, polishing their gear, sewing on buttons, writing letters home, bathing, and washing clothes in the creek. Al spent a great deal of time practicing the many distinct staccato beats that transmitted orders to marching men. Written instructions were not available to Al, nor would he have known how to read drum music. He learned by listening intently to the other drummers in the regiment, who already knew the commands. Someone told Al that a crack regiment was one that could Dress Parade all over a parade ground with no spoken orders, the signals given entirely by the drums. To do this became Al's ambition.

Military drum music can be heard on <www.militaryheritage.com/sound.htm> and <www.usmilitary.about.com.htm>.

Before the age of electronic communications, bugles and drums were used to communicate in camp and on the battlefield. Al's drum was an essential part of the drill and discipline that made an effective military unit. His company had to recognize the various beats as well, and no one was more frustrated than Al when

Camp life

Company C disintegrated into a stumbling, confused mass because the raw recruits mixed up his commands. He ground his teeth and stamped his feet and cursed the fact that he wasn't big enough to scold them.

Sketch of a drummer boy by Edwin Forbes, a nineteenth-century artist whose drawings appeared in Leslie's Illustrated Newspaper. *Morgan collection of Civil War drawings, Library of Congress LC-DIG-ppmsca-20545.*

Al's day began at 5:00 a.m., which at first seemed like an ungodly hour to roll out of his blanket. But Reveille had to be sounded at 5:15. At 5:30, Assembly call brought the company into formation for roll call. Al's day went like this:

- 5:15 Reveille: Soldiers got up, put on boots, straightened uniforms, and lined up for roll call.
- 5:30 Assembly: Each company formed in line and the first sergeant called the roll. The sergeant then reported to his company commander the number of men in camp, the number sick, the number present for duty, the number in special detail, and the number AWOL (absent without leave).
- Breakfast Call: Soldiers prepared their own breakfast. Or if in regular quarters, each man took his plate and tin cup and received his allotted ration, already cooked, from the company cook.
- Sick Call: Those who were sick reported to the surgeon's quarters or hospital tent.
- Fatigue Call: Men detailed to fatigue duty policed the camp or performed other assigned duties.
- Guard Mount: Inspection.
- Drill Call: Company drill.
- Noon Recall.
- Dinner Call.
- Assembly Call for regimental drill.
- 4:00 p.m. Assembly Call for Dress Parade at 5:00.
- Supper Call.
- 9:00 p.m. Roll Call.
- Retreat.
- 10:00 p.m. Tattoo.

Fatigue detail or fatigue duty was any task not requiring soldiers to stand formation, such as policing the camp or unloading supplies.

An infantry company falls in beside their camp.
Mathew Brady Photographs of Civil War-Era Personalities and Scenes, National Archives 111-B-273.

Every night Al beat Tattoo, indicating the time to return to quarters for the night. Finally a nearby bugler sounded Taps, initiated in 1862 to call for lights out.

Al also had to know the calls for special events: Boots and Saddles (breaking camp); The General (strike tents and be prepared to march); Assembly (companies form); To the Colors (covers off battle flags); and Parley (arrange negotiations). In battle, the drums beat both Charge! and Retreat!

The preliminary Emancipation Proclamation, issued on September 22, 1862, was to take effect on January 1, 1863. All the men were discussing what effect it would have on Northern sentiments. Slavery was not what had motivated these western volunteers to enlist, for they had had little contact with slaves. They had enlisted to save the Union, or because they had been swept up in the excitement of drums and bugles and cheering crowds, or perhaps just for a lark. Al listened without really understanding what slavery had to do with him. The only slave he'd ever seen up close was one who slid into camp one night, seeking protection and safety. He had no idea

President Lincoln's Emancipation Proclamation declared that slaves in Confederate States were henceforth free.

how a presidential proclamation freeing Southern slaves would affect the outcome of the war.

On October 6, 1862, the Seventy-fifth struck their tents in Louisville and marched to Frankfort, Kentucky, where Jacob Lair fell ill with a high fever. He was sick enough that Al and his comrades worried when Jacob doggedly got back on his feet to march with the regiment to Scottsville, Kentucky.[5]

The information about Jacob's illness in Frankfort comes from an affidavit in his pension file, written in 1902 by Albert Walton (Almon Beneway). The affidavit is quoted in full in a sidebar in the Afterword of this book. Piecing together these bits of information is a little like doing a jigsaw puzzle.

Four inches of snow fell on October 25, 1862. On October 26 the regiment struck their tents and followed the Kentucky River on the north side. They covered 19 miles that day, but the slippery snow made marching difficult. When they stopped to rest, they spread their oilcloth ponchos to sit on. When they finally stopped to bivouac, Al felt more tired than he had ever been. He had seen some of the men drop out of line, too weary to keep up.

Wet feet in stiff, ill-fitting army boots meant blisters. Al and Jacob debated whether to take off their boots to air the blisters, but agreed that their feet would freeze if they walked around in snow. As they chewed their hardtack, they watched the stragglers come into camp and grumble that they were all about as miserable as they had ever been.

Although Al and Jacob spread both their ponchos; the snow under them made a bitterly cold bed. Fortunately there were always two or three men with an ax or a hatchet, who headed for the nearest woods and brought back armloads of saplings. If a huge bonfire was kept roaring through the night, the soldiers could go out two or three times and warm up enough to sleep again.

Another drummer boy, Henry Martyn Kieffer (mentioned in Chapter 2), recalled "those weird night scenes of army life—the blazing fire, the groups of swarthy men gathered about, the thick darkness of the forest, where the lights and shadows danced and played all night long, and the rows of little white tents, covered with frost . . .."[6]

Camp life

Al was not aware that in Company K of his own regiment, Corporal William Bluffton Miller was keeping a journal that told of their daily activities. On October 31 Corporal Miller wrote, "We marched twenty two days in this month and upwards of three hundred miles." On November 5 he noted that "the fences have all been burned by the two Armies and it makes it look desolate."[7] Private Kieffer also wrote about the rail fences: "To make a fire was a comparatively easy matter, notwithstanding the rain; for some one or other always had matches, and there were plenty of rails at hand, and these were dry enough when split open with a hatchet or an ax. In a few moments the fence around the cornfield was carried off, rail by rail, and everywhere was heard the sound . . . of roaring campfires . . .".[8] The rail fences were also speedily torn apart to build defensive breastworks behind which the troops could shelter as they waited for an enemy attack.

Breastworks were temporary fortifications, usually of earth and about chest high, over which a soldier could fire.

As a result of losing the battle of Perrysville on October 8, the two Confederate armies of General Bragg and General Smith gave up their thrust deep into Kentucky, rendezvoused at Hodgenville, and retreated through the Cumberland Gap to eastern Tennessee. Angered by General Buell's unenthusiastic pursuit of the Confederates, President Lincoln replaced Buell on October 24 with General William S. Rosecrans.

On November 6 General William S. Rosecrans and General Dumont reviewed the regiment. Al was only vaguely aware of how these dashing men on horseback, wearing stiff uniforms with brass buttons and gold braid, fit into the scheme of things. Think of the excitement that he and the other drummers and buglers felt as they formed the troops in open order for review.

The general "is a fine looking military man and makes a fine appearance on horseback. . . . he road [sic] down in our front and back in the rear while we Stood at 'Parade Rest.' We did not get relieve [sic] untill [sic] nearly dark and did not get supper untill long after dark."[9]

Major General William S. Rosecrans, commander of the Army of the Cumberland. Library of Congress LC-B8172-2001.

Miller reported that the troops were issued shoes on November 7, pantaloons and dress coats on November 10.[10] His regular Sunday routine included doing his washing, cleaning his gun, and patching his clothes. In late November they moved on to Gallatin, Tennessee, where Private Mark Cox of Company C died. Al played dirges with a muffled drum at the funerals of his comrades. These deaths made Al even more anxious about Jacob's health.

On December 4 Miller mentioned "a quite cold and heavy frost last night."[11] On December 7 General Morgan's Confederate cavalry launched a surprise attack on the Federal brigade encamped near Hartsville, Tennessee. The Seventy-fifth quickly formed ranks and set off to render assistance. Al's captain ordered the company to march double-quick, mostly in Line of Battle, over fences and hills, through ravines and fields. Al beat the quickened pace with mounting excitement. The morning was chilly—a little snow had fallen during the night.[12] Corporal Miller wrote that "the Snow and Ice made it hard marching."[13]

Each company arranged its troops in a set order, as did the ranks of the whole regiment. Otherwise total confusion would have occurred each time they were ordered to Fall In.

Supplies were brought to the troops in quartermaster wagons. Mathew Brady Photographs of Civil War-Era Personalities and Scenes, National Archives 111-B-766.

The fight was over when the Seventy-fifth arrived. Returning to their own camp in Gallatin, they began reinforcing their fortifications against such an attack.

Much of December 1862 was passed in Gallatin, Tennessee, and later, in January 1863, a winter camp was established in Murfreesboro, Tennessee, where Jacob had time to fully recover. Al and his company constructed log cabins with canvas ceilings and a chimney for a stove. Some of the soldiers built complete log cabins, roof and all, which were a relief because their Sibley tents had been pitched and taken down so often that they were torn and leaking. Latrines were dug close to the streams that served both for bathing and drinking water.

Poor sanitation in crowded army camps was a major cause of illness. Soldiers' blankets were soon dirty. They all wore the same filthy, sweat-stained woolen uniform day and night for months at a time, with only the occasional change of shirt and underclothing. Some men tried much harder than others to keep clean, washing when water was available. Others didn't care. More than two dozen soldiers from the

Soldiers build a cabin for winter quarters. Mathew Brady Photographs of Civil War-Era Personalities and Scenes, National Archives 111-B-262.

Seventy-fifth Indiana Infantry Volunteers died of disease that winter. At least nine members died of disease at Louisville, including Private John Fay and Private Allen M. Poff of Company C.

Every soldier had body lice and fleas, which carried and spread disease. Because it was utterly impossible to be free of them, initial disgust gave way to hardened indifference. Al learned to hold his shirt over a campfire, where the heat made the lice fall into the fire, making a sound like popping corn. He and his buddies also picked up chiggers, wood ticks, and sand fleas, which caused endless itching.

As the coffins were buried one by one, Al realized that disease was killing more soldiers than bullets. Even men accustomed to physical labor found their endurance sorely taxed by long marches, inadequate rations, and the discomfort of life in the open. Without fresh fruit or vegetables or fresh meat, health deteriorated. Dozens

Camp life

of soldiers succumbed to typhoid, dysentery, or measles, or went home invalided with rheumatism, diarrhea, or general debility. Of course, there were always some malingerers who feigned illness to escape drill or fatigue duty.

The monotonous drudgery of army life, with its ceaseless round of drills, guard duty, and fatigue details, tested the morale of even the most patriotic volunteers. The physical discomfort was compounded by boredom. Morale was also tested by a few uncouth recruits whose foul language and negative attitude marred the atmosphere for their fellows. Al escaped them by practicing his drum rolls, running each one over in his mind—the call to roll out in the morning and come to meals, and all the various military commands. Captain Bryant emphasized how vital it was that Company C hear his commands while they were on the march. Total confusion would result if they heard the beat of a different drummer.

Occasionally the principal drummer of the regiment, Abner W. Ross, summoned the 13 musicians in the regiment to practice together so that they would be proficient when the regiment did Dress Parade with the line of drums out in front. What a glorious sound that was. Everyone who heard them felt his heart beat faster. Al also carried water buckets for his company and shaved some of them. Captain Bryant had him practice drawing simple maps of the surrounding countryside—roads, trees, fields, streams, houses—to prepare him for performing that task during later campaigns. And the regimental surgeon, Christopher S. Arthur, showed all the musicians how to clean and sharpen surgical instruments and how to compress an artery, apply a tourniquet (or make one from a handkerchief), put on bandages, and carry men in litters to the waiting ambulances. Dr. Arthur explained that during combat Al and the others would be sent to the field hospital. "You can assist me at the operating table, or go to the front with a stretcher to bring in the wounded. You

Soldiers at ease by their tents. The man in the middle holds a hand-cranked ice cream freezer. The soldier standing on the left has a bayonet on his rifle, while the soldier on the right does not. Mathew Brady Photographs of Civil War-Era Personalities and Scenes, National Archives 111-B-5548.

Camp life

may have to help hold soldiers down during amputations, or bury amputated limbs afterwards."

Other soldiers relieved boredom in any way they could. They organized competitions—pitching horseshoes, racing on foot and with wheelbarrows, climbing a greased pole, running after a soaped pig. On a sunny day a baseball game was always in progress. Some of the soldiers boxed. Men carried playing cards, dice, chessmen, and checkerboards in their knapsacks. They played poker in marathon sessions.

Books and newspapers were passed from hand to hand. Letter writing helped to pass the time. Al watched in silence as his companions cheered the arrival of the regimental postmaster. Soldiers gathered eagerly about the captain's tent while the names were being called. A letter from home was a delight. A package containing edibles was a huge treat.

A camp scene with soldiers taking their ease, playing cards in the foreground. Mathew Brady Photographs of Civil War-Era Personalities and Scenes, National Archives 111-B-275.

A mail wagon in 1863. This is a copy of a drawing on page 116, Volume I, Army and Navy of the United States, *in the Quartermaster Corps Library. Mathew Brady Photographs of Civil War-Era Personalities and Scenes, National Archives 111-B-2120.*

When Al was far enough away from home that his mother couldn't come after him, he broke down and wrote to her, telling her where he was. He must have sent her the photo that is on the cover of this book. Probably he also sent her part or all of his $12 monthly salary.[14]

Many of the men whittled rings for their loved one at home, using their soft lead bullets. They had mock sword fights. They played practical jokes. They played musical instruments—violins, flutes, harmonicas, banjos, and accordions were found in every regiment. Singers formed quartets and glee clubs.

It was a hard-drinking era, and liquor was very bad for discipline. The officers tried to thwart the drinking, but the troops invariably evaded their efforts. They smuggled kegs of beer and jugs of whiskey into camp. Even bottles of patent medicine, containing mostly alcohol, were sought after.

Camp life

A card game outside a winter camp. The drummer boy has parked his drum under their table. Mathew Brady Photographs of Civil War-Era Personalities and Scenes, National Archives 111-B-293.

Chapter 3 Endnotes

[1] *History*, pp. 25-26.

[2] *History*, p. 24.

[3] William Bluffton Miller's service record indicates that he was 23 years old, 5 feet 10 1/2 inches tall, with a fair complexion, blue eyes, and light-colored hair.

[4] "The Civil War Diary of William Bluffton Miller," edited by Jeffrey L. Patrick and Robert J. Willey, published under the title of *Fighting for Liberty and the Right* (University of Tennessee Press, 2005), pp. 75-76.Corporal Miller was injured in the Battle of Chickamauga. He returned to his regiment after he recovered and was promoted to sergeant on May 3, 1864. Hereafter referred to as "Miller."

[5] A half dozen men died in Scottsville, including Private Henry Jones from Al's own Company C.

[6] Kieffer, Henry Martyn, *The Recollections of a Drummer Boy* (Boston: Ticknor and Company, 1889). Reproduced by the Library of Congress, 2010, p. 162.

[7] Miller, p. 17.

[8] Kieffer, p. 77.

[9] Miller, p. 37.

[10] Miller, p.37.

[11] Miller, p. 45.

[12] *History*, p. 51.

[13] Miller, p. 46.

[14] Information about a musician's salary came from Revised United States Army Regulations of 1861 with an Appendix containing the Changes and Laws Affecting Army Regulations and Articles of War to June 25, 1863, issued by the U.S. War Department (Washington: Government Printing Office, 1863). Available on the University of Michigan Library website <http://quod.lib.umich.edu/> and confirmed in Al's memoir.

CHAPTER 4   "Scouting expeditions and marches"

Almon was around 70 when he wrote his memoir, and what he remembered in his old age was his prison experience. He summed up a whole year of military duty in a single sentence: "I was in a great many scouting expeditions and marches." Fortunately, a member of his regiment, Corporal William Bluffton Miller of Company K, kept a diary[1] which permits the reconstruction of what happened between September 1862, when Al was mustered in, and September 1863, when he was captured at Chickamauga.

In that first year of Al's active duty the Seventy-fifth Indiana Infantry Volunteers played an active part in the campaign for control of the Memphis and Charleston Railroad. This took them to many parts of Kentucky and Tennessee in pursuit of Morgan's forces. At times the Confederate cavalry was so close that Union pickets could hear the sound of horses' hoofs in the night. Most nights Al and his buddies were ordered to "sleep on arms," some lying on rocks, some sitting bolt upright against tree trunks, some stretched out on beds of moss or under clumps of bushes, caps shielding their faces if it was raining. Al knew that sleeping out on the ground was not helping Jacob's recovery. Nor was rising at 3 o'clock in the morning to stand in the Line of Battle until the rising sun made any enemy visible and ended their vigil against a sudden onslaught. Though they were not attacked, the discipline taught them to be alert at all times.

> Line of Battle was a long line four or five men deep in which a regiment advanced against the enemy.

General Bragg's Confederate army was estimated at 43,000 men; their supplies were stored at Tullahoma. In October 1862, when Major General W.S. Rosecrans replaced General Buell as commander, the Federal army was renamed the Army of the Cumberland. It numbered about 65,000 men as it prepared to advance against Bragg. Al couldn't visualize that many men operating under one command. It was hard to visualize 400 - 500 men in a regiment, but Rosecrans's army comprised the equivalent of 65 regiments. Of course, some of the units were cavalry, some were batteries of cannon, and some were pickets or skirmishers.

The Army of the Cumberland consisted of five corps, which included 14 divisions made up of 38 brigades. Each brigade comprised three to five regiments. All these units were under the command of one man, who passed his orders to the officers commanding each unit, who in turn passed their commands down to the officers of the smaller units. Al and his comrades had no idea how the strategy for a battle was worked out. All they knew was that when the orderlies rode in with messages, their captain gave the order to move, Al beat his drum roll, and they moved. And they sang "Rally round the flag, boys, rally once again, shouting the battle cry of freedom."

Christmas 1862 was spent in Gallatin, Tennessee. The men had only their usual rations of hardtack and salt pork for Christmas dinner, made palatable by placing a thin slice of meat and a spoonful of brown sugar on top of the dry cracker. Their shelter tents were pitched on hard, frozen ground. Needless to say, most of the

The officers of the Army of the Cumberland meet to discuss strategy. Mathew Brady Photographs of Civil War-Era Personalities and Scenes, National Archives 111-B-7030.

"Scouting expeditions and marches"

men spent Christmas Eve crowded around the campfires, smoking their pipes, telling yarns, singing until far into the night.

January brought more cold and snow. Al found it hard to control his drumbeats when his fingers were stiff with cold. His first months in the army had been far more demanding than he had ever anticipated. Company C was his whole life now. When he was not busy with his own duties, he shadowed Jacob, searching for small tasks that he could perform for him.

In early January 1863 the regiment guarded a train of 1,500 wagons carrying supplies to the front for the troops who had survived the fierce, three-day battle of Stones River near Murfreesboro, Tennessee. Rumors were soon circulating among the troops that, during the battle, General Rosecrans had ridden furiously through the worst of the enemy cannon fire from one front-line unit to another, a cigar stub clenched in his teeth, advising and encouraging his hard-pressed troops.

As they marched under the rattle of musket fire, the Seventy-fifth met ambulances conveying the wounded to Nashville, Tennessee. At night the troops stopped where they stood, moved off the road, and lay down in the bushes, wrapped in their oilcloth ponchos to ward off the rain. When the Seventy-fifth Indiana arrived on the field at Stones River during the morning of January 7, 1863, the noise of the conflict had ceased and the smoke of battle cleared away. Al looked at the dead men and torn and mangled horses, the broken cannon carriages and wheels strewn over the field. He smelled

Musket: A smoothbore, muzzle-loading gun shot with the barrel resting against the shoulder.

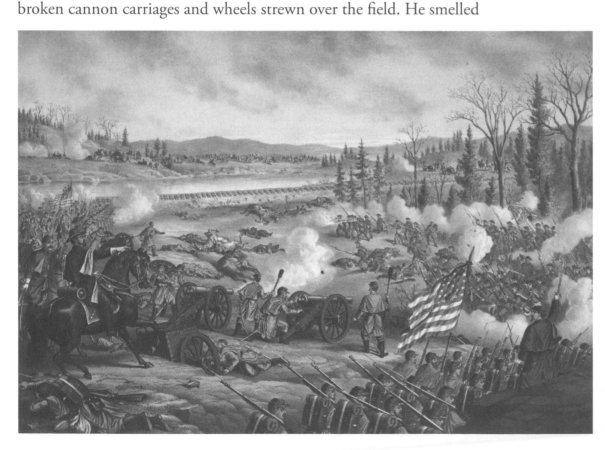

A lithograph of the battle of Stones River, near Murfreesboro, Tennessee, December 31, 1862, January 2-3, 1863. Library of Congress LC-DIG-pga-01858.

"Scouting expeditions and marches"

the stench of blood and excrement, swallowed hard, and clenched his teeth to keep from gagging. He didn't know what a heroic battlefield should look like, but the carnage spread out before him was not what he had expected.

Bragg's defeated Confederate army went into winter quarters at Shelbyville and Tullahoma. The Seventy-fifth camped at Murfreesboro until June 24, serving in General Joseph J. Reynolds's division, and engaging in scouting and other arduous duty.

Murfreesboro had bakeries that could supply soft bread—a real treat for hungry troops. Corporal Miller chanced to "see the pile of Hard Tack at the Depot. I thought there was grub to last a long time but when you look around and see the Soldiers I come to the conclusion that it would soon disappear. . . ."[2]

On March 30 Corporal Miller wrote that they were ordered to prepare for a Grand Review the next day. "We did not get out of camp until noon as other Troops were moveing [sic] and occupied the road. Our entire Division was out. We were formed by Regiments in open order. General Rosecrans and escort rode to the left in front and back in the rear of us and then we 'closed up' and formed in column by company and marched by the Generals. It was a nice Show but I got very tired marching. We returned to camp and Stacked Arms on color line and policed our quarters So if General Rosecrans rode through the camp it would look clean. But they did not visit our camp. If they were as tired as we are they were glad to get into quarters and don't care whether our camp is clean or not."[4]

Al was distressed when Corporal James Oldham of Company C died of heart disease at Murfreesboro on April 2, 1863. More than 30 soldiers of the Seventy-fifth died while they were camped at Murfreesboro, including two other men from

"Murfreesboro was a handsome, educational town, built chiefly of brick, lighted with gas, containing 3500 inhabitants, half a dozen churches, two female colleges, a university and a military institute. It was located on an elevated plain, beautiful for situation, near the spurs of the Cumberland Mountains. Stone's River, on the banks of which the great battle was fought, flowed on the west side of town.

"The encampment of the 75th Indiana Volunteers . . . was located on the east side of the town . . . It was made very nice and cleanly [sic] and healthy by the removal of all rubbish and decaying vegetation. It was laid out city fashion, into company streets, by the formation of the tents into straight and regular rows. They used the conical Sibley tent, with the base of the circle fastened to the ground by wooden pegs. These tents held from 25 to 30 men, sleeping in a circle."[3]

Al's own Company C, Private George Henderson and Private Jacob Hinkle. They were put into rough coffins and hauled to ground chosen as a cemetery, buried by men detailed for that purpose. A little board was set up at each man's head with the number of the grave put on it, but no words to tell who the soldier was or where he came from. With a single drumstick, Al beat his drum slowly as each wrapped body was carried from wagon to freshly dug grave. Then he listened to the quiet voice of the chaplain: "The Lord is my shepherd, I shall not want . . .." At the end, the triple notes of Taps seemed to echo Al's dismay at how slight his buddies' hold on life had been.

During this time the Seventy-fifth served in the Second Brigade, Fourth Division, Fourteenth Army Corps. It was known as the "Indiana Brigade," being composed of the Seventy-fifth, Eighty-eighth, and One Hundred First Indiana, and One Hundred Fifth Ohio regiments. Its overall mission was to seize control of the Nashville and Chattanooga Railroad to prevent Confederate supplies from reaching their destination. The brigade made several forays, Al leading his company each time. They engaged Confederate troops, capturing 47 and destroying several Confederate supply trains. They also rounded up 300 horses and mules and 50 head of beef cattle, which would supply the delicacy of fresh meat to hungry troops. In a later expedition the brigade destroyed railroad bridges and trestles, burning an engine, train of cars, and the depot at McMinnville. They burned a large cotton factory and three mills and captured 180 prisoners and 613 animals.

Spring came earlier here than it did in Indiana. Al noticed wildflowers blooming beside the road and flowering bushes in the hedgerows. Peach orchards were clouds of pink blossom, and by May the smell of honeysuckle was in the air. Some of the boys boxed up their overcoats and sent them home; they were a nuisance to carry when they were not needed. Some of the soldiers got in trouble for not carrying their cartridge boxes during Drill. Forty rounds of ammunition were heavy and the boxes cumbersome, but leaving them behind could be disastrous in battle.

"Scouting expeditions and marches"

Men with a rough shelter they have constructed. Mathew Brady Photographs of Civil War-Era Personalities and Scenes, National Archives 111-B-5508.

On May 1 the number of wagon trains each regiment was entitled to was reduced from 13 wagons to three. One way of greatly reducing their load was to discard the old Sibley tents, which held 25 men, replacing them with shelter tents. Each soldier carried half of a tent in his knapsack. Two soldiers would button their halves together to create a dog tent or pup tent. A tree limb served as ridge pole. If no limbs were available, the men used their muskets to improvise support. Men who were bivouacked on outpost duty made shelters called "shebangs," constructed of tree branches leaning on a transverse pole.

An infantry camp of Sibley tents. Mathew Brady Photographs of Civil War-Era Personalities and Scenes, National Archives 111-B-449.

Al was elated when Jacob Lair said he was to share his tent. It seemed like an extraordinary affirmation of friendship. Only later, when several privates suggested the same thing, commenting that he wouldn't take up much room in a shelter tent, did Al realize that his small size was his main attraction.

On May 20, 1863, Corporal Miller wrote that General Rosecrans appeared again for Battalion Drill and Brigade Drill. Al particularly enjoyed Brigade Drill because the brigade had a band, and a little stirring music enlivened the drills for everyone.

On May 23 Colonel Hall conducted Brigade Inspection and Dress Parade. On May 25 General Joseph J. Reynolds came for the regiment's Battalion Drill and Dress Parade. "Genl Reynolds dismounted at Guard House and played with Little Al, drummer Boy of company C. He is a nice friendly old gentleman. He does not think it a disgrace to talk to a private Soldier like a great many men of less rank."[5]

Corporal Miller's reaction to the general is amusing. Al must have been astonished to receive personal attention from the commanding general.

> Al and Jacob's close friendship is revealed in two affidavits Al wrote in Jacob's behalf in 1901 and 1902. They can be found in the Afterword of this book.

"Scouting expeditions and marches"

Major General Joseph J. Reynolds, who dismounted to talk to Al during a review of the troops. Portrait by Alden Finney Brooks, Library of Congress LC-DIG-ppmsca-22323.

On May 30 Corporal Miller made finger rings for his wife and sister, using mussel shells from Stones River. "The shells are very nice and resemble Ivory and are hard. Our Boys manufacture lots of little tokens from them."[6]

On June 4 the troops were ordered to draw eight days' rations, packing five into their knapsacks and three into their haversacks. The order made them think some sort of action was imminent. Nothing happened. On June 8 they formed for Officers Drill and Regimental Inspection. Corporal Miller wrote that "another Brigade joined our Division. We are now the Second Brigade Fourth Division and Fourteenth Army Corps under General Gco. H. Thomas or 'Pap' Thomas as he is called. Genl Thomas is a very large man, will weigh about two hundred & twenty five pounds. About fifty years old and makes a fine appearance and our Boys think there is nobody like him. I always hear men speak of him with praise and we are proud to be led by him."[7]

When orders came to break winter camp, the men had to abandon surplus baggage they had collected during the winter. On June 24 the Seventy-fifth started toward Tullahoma during a downpour, marching in slippery mud. They sang to keep up their spirits. "Tramp, tramp, tramp, the boys are marching, Cheer up, comrades, they will come . . .."

The supply train got bogged down, and Al and several of his comrades went off to forage for chickens, eggs, turkeys, corn, sweet potatoes, pigs, and whatever else they could find. Generals issued stern orders against looting and robbery, but these volunteer soldiers and their volunteer officers paid little attention after they got into enemy country. They gathered firewood and corn and hay for the officers' horses. They searched for dairies for cheese and smokehouses for hams and shoulders. Blackberries grew along the roadsides. The soldiers ate them even though they were barely ripe, and some suffered stomach cramps.

Foraging in the countryside "... was just what was bound to happen in a civil war in nineteenth-century America. The rowdy strain was coming up to the surface again; as it had been called upon to help create the war, and there was no way to repress it ....An army of invasion composed of volunteers who considered themselves free citizens despite their uniforms and their oaths of enlistment was going 'to use this country rough,' and that was that."[8]

Chattanooga was Bragg's principal base of supplies. Although parts of his army, at different times, were sent out in various directions on reconnoitering expeditions, all the Northern troops were anxiously awaiting a general movement against Bragg. Union General Rosecrans could not advance except through the passes between the high hills that Bragg's army held. The country roads, soaked in ankle-deep mud, were in a terrible condition for the movement of a vast army.

Rosecrans decided to make Bragg think he would be advancing from Murfreesboro toward Shelbyville, but he intended to turn Bragg's right flank and move to his rear by sending a large part of his army through Hoover's Gap, a narrow valley five miles long between high hills.

When on June 24 orders came finally to march, the Seventy-fifth headed for Hoover's Gap, where they first "'saw the elephant"—soldiers' slang for baptism by fire. At his captain's command Al sounded out the long drum roll that meant Forward March. Captain Bryant told him to beat his drum in double time because they were in a hurry. Al grinned with excitement as they set off.

Fifteen hundred mounted horsemen led the way, galloping full tilt through the gap, chasing surprised Confederate pickets before them and overrunning a camp of Confederate cavalry, who scattered into the woods. The Federal infantry following them were to move at top speed through the narrow defile in the mountains, while skirmishers engaged the surprised Confederates on either side. Al heard the rattle of small-arms fire mingling with blasts of artillery. Horse-drawn cannon were stationed on the mountainsides, pointing down the road, with too few men assigned to man them. Sharpshooters picked them off one by one. Broken-down Confederate wagons and discarded food and clothing littered the roadside.

> Artillery are large-caliber weapons that are too heavy to carry and are served by crews. These units of men, trained to place and fire cannon during battle, had to have an understanding of distance and trajectories. The cannon were moved by horses.

Corporal Miller described that day in his diary: "We had marched about Seventeen miles and had filed off the road to camp when the firing in front commenced. We were ordered on to the scene of action and formed Line of Battle and drove the Enemy back and occupied the position in Hoover's Gap. The Battle was spirited while it lasted. It appears the Rebels were being reviewed at War Trace or Manchester by Bragg and left only a few men to Guard this place and Colonel John T. Wilder's Lightning Brigade drove them out and pursued them some distance and then re-inforcements comeing [sic] up Wilder fell back here and we come in time to assist him and we hold the position with the enemy in our front. . . . We were called out at two o'clock am for Picket and I think it is the darkest night I ever seen. It rained very hard. We kept together by holding to our File Leader's coat tail. We could hear the wounded lying on the Battle field calling for help but we could not get to them."[9]

Confederate reinforcements arrived in time to stem the flow of Federal troops through the gap. With the marching infantry pinned down, fighting continued for two days until the Confederates finally withdrew. The men of the Seventy-fifth Indiana not only "saw the elephant," they had a real baptism by fire. Two men from the Seventy-fifth were wounded along the way: Isaac Pitzer of Company B was shot in the face and Cyrus V. Gorrell of Company K lost an eye. A number of men died at

Hoover's Gap, including Regimental Chaplain John R. Eddy. Al was a much sobered boy when orders came to march again.

Bragg retreated to Tullahoma, pursued by Federal troops. Corporal Miller expressed their apprehensions: "Who can describe their feelings advanceing [sic] on a line where he expects every Step will bring death and destruction all around. But we crawled on and under and over the timber and the large guns frowning on us from the works. But we reach the works and find that the enemy is gone and with a Shout we mount and turn and look back and see our Regiment in the first line and One Battalion after another to the right and left as far as the eye can see and behind them the 1st and 2nd lines in battle array comeing [sic] on. When we mount the works the Adjutant comes down the road with our flag and we rush into town and plant it on the fort an[d] on the highest hill. Then we lay down on the hill and watch the advance of the Army and fineally [sic] they file off in the different roads and march into town. The 75th is the first Regiment in Side [sic] of the Rebel works. That is glory enough for one day, but I am very tired."[10]

Al and his comrades picked their way through Confederate fortifications of felled trees, their sharpened ends directed upwards and outwards toward the enemy. The rain still came down incessantly, streams were swollen too deep to ford, bridges had been destroyed. The mud was so deep that it came over the tops of their boots. That night Al listened to C Company officers bragging that the 10-day campaign had forced the Confederates out of all the important territory north of the Tennessee River. Having sent their knapsacks back to Murfreesboro to lighten their loads, the troops had marched 70 miles, on railroad tracks some of the way, pushed successfully through Hoover's Gap, slept in the rain, gone hungry when their wagon trains were mired in mud, and waded rivers and streams without a dry stitch of clothing. Al learned that the smart soldier carried several day's rations in his haversack, because even the sutlers—traveling vendors who offered food like sausages or sardines for sale at very high prices—couldn't keep up with a marching army.

Facing page: Sketch of drummer boys by Edwin Forbes. Part of "Life studies of the great army," Morgan collection of Civil War drawings, Library of Congress LC-DIG-ppmsca-20761.

"Scouting expeditions and marches"

Drummer boys.

Drummer Boy of Company C

While his companions were with great difficulty keeping their powder dry, Al put just as much effort into protecting his drum head. Now all he wanted was hot food and shelter from the rain. They were much sobered and chastened by what they had experienced, knowing now that war was not glory and heroics. War was dodging bullets and slogging through mud.

Two more men of the Seventy-fifth died of disease at Tullahoma in July 1863: James S. Wilson of Company K and Artilleus Biddle of Company I. On the 4th of July the troops were elated to hear that Union armies had turned back General Robert E. Lee's Confederate army at Gettysburg the day before.

Corporal Miller went gathering "huckle berries." On July 6 he noted that they were short of rations, so "Some of us went out to forage. We got a Calf and a good hog (Strays) and Supplied us with meat. The sun shone very hot." On July 7 they heard that Vicksburg had surrendered to General Grant "and Several guns were fired in honor of the victories by our Batteries."[11] On July 8 their wagon trains with their rations caught up with them. On July 19 they gathered a half bushel of apples and a half gallon of berries. Finally they could fill their gnawing stomachs.

On August 16 General Rosecrans's Army of the Cumberland, having halted its pursuit of Bragg's Army of Tennessee at the foot of the Cumberland plateau to rest, refit, and restore service on the Nashville and Chatanooga Railroad as far forward as the Cowan Tunnel, resumed offensive operations.

Bragg fell back to Chattanooga. On a hot, dry day in late August, the Seventy-fifth Regiment marched for miles along the backbone of a chain of mountains in blazing sun. Al's water canteen was soon emptied, but there was no source of water along the line of march. The hundreds of marching feet stirred up clouds of dry dust, parching Al's lips and making breathing difficult. Strong men fainted by the wayside. Al breathed a sigh of relief when in late afternoon they reached Battle Creek. A squad from the Seventy-fifth was sent to destroy the railroad bridge nearby. They found Confederate soldiers busy destroying the other end of the bridge. It took seven days

"Scouting expeditions and marches"

Constructing a pontoon bridge across a river. Civil War-Era Photographs, National Archives 111-BA-59.

for the Army of the Cumberland to build pontoon bridges and cross the Tennessee River. On August 30 the Indiana Brigade crossed on eight flat boats that they had constructed or captured.

CHAPTER 4 ENDNOTES

[1] *Fighting for Liberty and the Right.*
[2] Miller, p. 82.
[3] *History*, pp. 65-66.
[4] Miller, p. 78.
[5] Miller, p. 93.
[6] Miller, p. 95.
[7] Miller, p. 97.
[8] Catton, p. 149.
[9] Miller, p. 103
[10] Miller, p. 107.
[11] Miller, p. 109.

Tintype image of Al holding a bugle. Al apparently folded the small metal plate into quarters and carried it with him during the war. Photo of original tintype on left and digitally enhanced version on right. Author's collection.

Cumberland Heights, Tennessee, seen from the Kentucky side. From a sketch by an engineer in the Confederate army published in Soldiers in Our Civil War. *Civil War-Era Photographs, National Archives 111-BA-2163.*

The battle of Chickamauga

CHAPTER 5   The battle of Chickamauga

After the Tullahoma campaign, General Rosecrans turned and split his three army corps, aiming to force the Confederates out of Chattanooga. They set out for Chattanooga by separate routes. Al and his regiment marched hard over two mountain chains and were exhausted. They were relieved then to spend several weeks in camp, doing vigorous drill and picket duty and training for battle.

Al's eyes sparkled as he saw fields of potatoes and ripe corn. Peach orchards hung heavy with fruit, and the hundreds of men climbing through the trees looked like flocks of starlings. What a splendid relief from weeks of eating hardtack. Trees and fields were stripped bare by the time the army moved on.

Al joined hundreds of men swimming in the Tennessee River. On September 1, Robert B. Commons of I Company had cramps and drowned. His comrades buried him with the honors of war beside the majestic stream. Al was reminded of his rescue a year earlier from the Potomac River.

In early September 1863 Rosecrans consolidated his forces scattered in Tennessee and Georgia and forced Bragg's army out of Chattanooga, heading south. The Union troops followed the retreating Confederates and brushed with them at Davis's Cross Roads. Bragg was determined to reoccupy Chattanooga, vital to his supply line, and decided to meet a part of Rosecrans's badly scattered army that was approaching from the north on a broad front, defeat them, and then move back into the city. On September 17 Bragg headed north. Rosecrans intended to beat him into Chattanooga. Al knew none of this, of course, only that they marched over a lot of rugged terrain.

The Union troops finally climbed Lookout Mountain, dragging all their artillery and wagons and equipment with them. And what a feat that was, everyone pulling and pushing and straining and struggling till they were drenched in sweat

A Union field hospital was located at Crawfish Springs. Mathew Brady Photographs of Civil War-Era Personalities and Scenes, National Archives 111-B-7026.

and breathing hard. It was a relief to reach Pond Spring, where they rested quietly for three days. On September 18 the Seventy-fifth marched four miles farther to Crawfish Springs, then continued their march into the night, racing to secure the road to Chattanooga.

"It was almost miraculous that during that fearful night they did not meet with some dreadful accidents. Here and there fences were set on fire, and the columns of marching troops, at one point, would penetrate the lurid light which illuminated their pathway, and at another would plunge into the impenetrable darkness. Hundreds of wagons, loaded with shells and powder, and immense trains of artillery,

The battle of Chickamauga

were compelled to pass over some of the burning rails, and intermingling with the marching infantry, choked up the narrow way. The deep dull rumbling of the artillery wagons, the clanking of arms, the thousands of subdued voices of men marching at midnight near the enemy, were ominous . . . ."[1]

As Bragg marched north on September 18, his cavalry and infantry fought with Union cavalry and mounted infantry armed with Spencer repeating rifles—devastating weapons because they fired half a dozen shots in a minute.

Bragg and his 66,000 men took positions on the west bank of Chickamauga Creek, an area of dense woods and thick underbrush. The Army of the Cumberland was spread along a front 42 miles in length, which could have been disastrous if General Bragg had immediately attacked. Fortunately he hesitated, while General Rosecrans set about consolidating his forces into a battle front six miles long.

General Thomas's Federal troops, the Seventy-fifth included, had marched all night and part of the day on roads so thick with dust that a marching column looked like a sandstorm. Al could hardly breathe, and his clothes and those of all his company were a uniform dusty brown color. When they reached Crawfish Springs, they learned that Bragg's vanguard had forced its way across Chickamauga Creek at Reed's Bridge.

Fighting began in earnest at dawn on the morning of September 19, as masses of infantry with flags flying moved out of the woods. Both sides were seeking control of the fords and bridges that crossed the creek.

Chickamauga is not a town, but rather a plain bordered on the west and north by Missionary Ridge, and on the east by Chickamauga Creek, from which the battle took its name. Chattanooga lies to the north.[2]

Captain James R. Carnahan, Eighty-sixth Indiana Infantry: "Scarce had our lines been formed, when the sharp crack of the rifles along our front and the whistling of balls over our heads, give us warning that the advance of the enemy has begun, and in an instant the shots of the skirmishers are drowned by the shout that goes up from the charging column as it starts down the woods. . . . The gunners and every man of those two batteries are at their posts of duty, the tightly drawn lines in their faces showing their purpose there to stand for duty or die. Officers pass the familiar command of caution along the line—'Steady, men, steady.' The shout of the charging foe comes rapidly on; now they burst out of the woods and onto the road. As if touched by an electric cord, so quick and so in unison was it, the rifles leap to the shoulder along the ridge where waves the stars and stripes. Now the enemy are in plain view along the road covering our entire front; you can see them, as with cap visors drawn well across their eyes, the gun at the charge, with short, shrill shouts they come, and we see their colors . . . . Just as that long line of gray has crossed the road, quick and sharp rings out along our line the command, 'Ready, Fire!' Again and again, with almost frightening rapidity, they pour in their deadly, merciless fire, until along that entire ridge it had become almost one continuous volley. . . . Again and again were those charges repeated along our line, only to be hurled back. . . ."[3]

When at 7:30 a.m. the first Confederate attack hit the extreme left of the Union battle front, Al was eating breakfast. He heard the first muttering of approaching conflict, the occasional boom of cannon, the irregular discharge of musketry. They were building a fire to boil coffee when the command to Fall In was given. Al grabbed his drum. The Seventy-fifth was moved to a position northeast of Widow Glenn's house. Shortly after noon they were wheeled into the Line of Battle. The Seventy-fifth Indiana Infantry and the Nineteenth Indiana Battery of artillery were posted as a reserve force on a slight ridge parallel to and east of the Chattanooga Road. The battery shot over the heads of the men in

A battery is the basic tactical artillery unit, corresponding to a company of infantry.

Looking across Chickamauga Creek toward Lookout Mountain. This is the terrain on which the battle was fought. Mathew Brady Photographs of Civil War-Era Personalities and Scenes, National Archives 111-B-1759.

The battle of Chickamauga

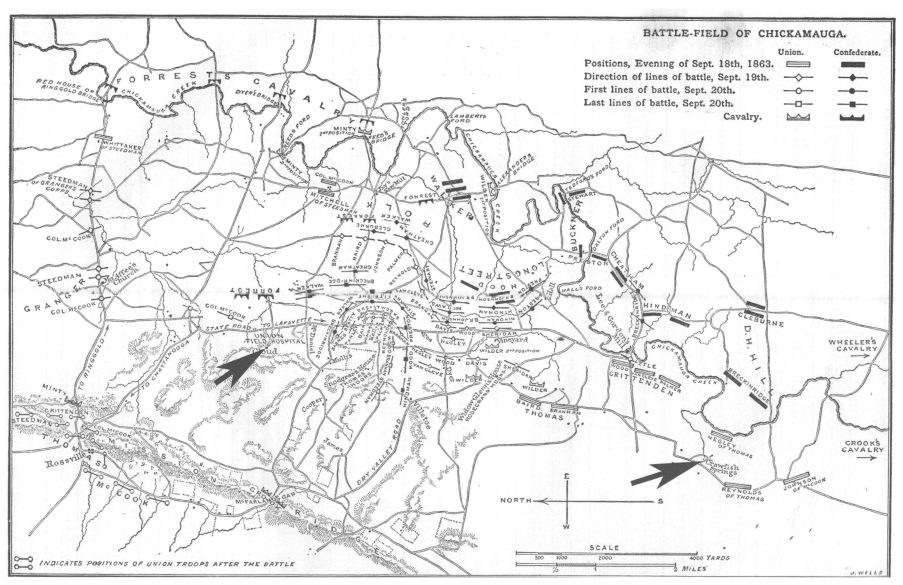

The field hospital at Cloud's farm house, where Al was captured, is located due north of the center of this map (see left arrow). The other field hospital, at Crawfish Springs, is on the lower right-hand side of this map (see right arrow). Battles and Leaders of the Civil War, *Volume III (New York: The Century Company, 1884), page 648.*

front, into the ranks of the enemy, with terrible effect. Sharpshooters picked off cannoneers and horses.

At 2:00 p.m. the Seventy-fifth was ordered forward to support the two Indiana batteries that were being assailed by Confederates. Al helped Private James E. Kidder of C Company, who had been shot through his shoulder, to the field hospital set up at Cloud's, a local farm house. The whole right side of Al's shirt was soon saturated with Kidder's warm blood. The front of the shirt, when Kidder's blood had dried on it, was as stiff as a board. Al had no other shirt. He had no idea that he would wear that same one for the months to come.

When Kidder had been placed in the row of wounded soldiers awaiting medical attention, Al turned away from the smell and noise of the building where the surgeons were operating. A pile of bloody arms and legs lay beneath the window. Al could see Surgeon Arthur inside, his coat off, sleeves rolled up to his elbows, shirt bespattered with blood, his sharp and glistening instrument in his hand. Al stumbled in his haste to leave the gory scene.

When Al tried to find his way back to his unit, they were not where he had left them. The smoke hung so heavy over the field that he couldn't tell friend from foe. He wandered back and forth, searching, dropping to the ground when shells whistled too close, peering into the brush and woods in search of a familiar face. It should have been easy, because every soldier wore the insignia of his company, number of his regiment, and symbol of his corps on the front or top of his forage cap. The different corps were distinguished by shapes, the different divisions by the colors of their badges, but the dust and smoke completely obscured even the colors of the uniforms. Al had no idea how much time passed while he was lost.

When he finally found his regiment across the field about 50 yards, behind an old worm-fence at the edge of the woods, he noticed that both the Stars and Stripes

Diary entry of Corporal William B. Miller, Company E, Seventy-fifth Indiana:

"The battle raged all day without ceasing until about five o'clock when I was struck by a Minnie [sic] Ball passing through my right thigh and lodging in my left one. It did not fracture the bone or knock me down but disabled me so I could not walk . . . . I managed to get back and Surgeon Dixon of the 1st Kentucky dressed it and ordered me off the field. I hobbled back and kept from being captured. Hamp Case the drummer Boy of my company came along with a Lieutenant who was wounded and he left him and took charge of me. Our men kept falling back as the Rebels pressed them and finally came out into the open field and from where I could see the battle. The Rebels seemed to be desperate. Some say they are drunk and they made one charge after another and the men made terrible havoc in their ranks. They kept up the fight until darkness put a stop to it. There was heavy fighting to our left until nine o'clock tonight. I was taken up about that time by the Ambulance train and taken to Crawfish Springs near where we had breakfasted this a.m. This has been a terrible day for the American nation and many bitter tears will be shed in the North and South for the dead of Chickamauga."[6]

The battle of Chickamauga

The examining surgeon's certificate describing the wounds received by Private James E. Kidder at the battle of Chickamauga. From Private Kidder's Pension File, National Archives.

Treating the wounded on the battlefield. Pencil drawing by Alfred R. Waud. From the Morgan collection of Civil War drawings, Library of Congress LC-USZC2-3821.

and the regimental battle flag were torn. Both flags had been rent by musket balls, and another piece of shell had struck the staff of the Stars and Stripes, badly marring it.

Several nearby units were running out of ammunition. The ammunition trains were supposedly parked in the woods to the rear, but finding them was difficult. When they retired for supply, the Seventy-fifth reformed and, holding its ground securely, was thrown into the breech. Orderlies went galloping past, delivering instructions from headquarters. Staff officers dashed up and down the line, seeing to it that orders were carried out. The battle carried on so long that dusk was falling, and there was confusion about unit positions and some doubt as to exactly where the enemy was.

Al and his comrades became aware that the officers leading them were uncertain where to establish their lines. The men muttered quietly in the dark. Seven men of the Seventy-fifth were buried hurriedly that night in rude graves, without coffin or ceremony.

The night was uncomfortably cold. Al's clothes were still damp from wading Chickamauga Creek the day before. The regiment stayed in the Line of Battle all night, the dead and wounded all about them. Surely some of Al's comrades asked him if he had heard about Sergeant Lair, and Al's heart must have dropped for fear his friend had been killed.

"No, no, he's all right. But he was a hero this afternoon." They told him that the color-bearer of his battle flag, Corporal James Stewart of F Company, was wounded in the right hip. As he fell, Color-Sergeant Jacob Lair, carrying the Stars and Stripes, seized the battle-flag as well, and being a muscular man, carried both flags as he heaved Corporal Stewart onto his back. In a few minutes a Minié ball pierced the body of Corporal Stewart from right to left immediately under his armpits as he hung bleeding and wounded on Color-Sergeant Lair's back. This shot killed the corporal. Corporal Thomas P. Henderson of C Company then seized the battle flag and carried it in honor to the close of the battle.[4]

Minié ball: Standard bullet-shaped projectile fired from the rifled muskets of the time. Designed by two French army officers, the bullet's hollow base expanded, forcing its sides into the grooves, or rifling, of the musket.

Al thought about this remarkable story long into the night. As they stood in the darkness, he could hear the wounded calling and begging for water. If troops tried to move about, they stumbled on dead men in the dark. The campfires cast their light over the ghastly scene, hundreds of corpses, mangled and torn, scattered around them. Al peered into the tangled, gloomy woodland. He looked at the stars barely penetrating the smoke above and the distant flickers from dead pine trees burning. Everything had a weird, ghostly appearance. In spite of the masses of men surrounding him, he felt very much alone.

The men were kept on their feet until 3:00 a.m., when they were allowed to rest and make fires. "The tired troops in their blue and gray uniforms went to sleep for a few hours on the gory field, with the expectation of the work of death to be continued by the coming of a new day. It came at last, red and sultry, with a dense fog and smoke hanging over the dead and dying of the previous day's battle . . .."[5]

At 9:30, the Confederates opened with an awful cannonade and musketry fire on the left of the Federal line. It swept along the front, causing brigades to shift and become muddled together. The Federal line was strengthened by a barricade of logs and rails, which each Division built in its immediate front during Saturday night and Sunday morning. Al and his company collected decaying logs and stumps and a few old rails, piling them up into a breastworks in front of their position. They were still building them on Sunday morning, after the battle on the left had fairly opened. During the construction of these works Lieutenant Colonel William O'Brien was wounded in the right forearm by buckshot.

Al's division was posted near the center of the Federal line. His brigade was slightly to the rear of the line on the left, facing Alexander's Bridge. The narrow road was covered ankle-deep with dust that rose in suffocating clouds. Al looked around him at Widow Kelly's field, in which the corn had been harvested but some corn-stalks were still standing. In this field also stood an old stump, and, during the succession of charges which the Confederates made, Al watched their flag fall several times as their color-bearers were shot. Finally they drove the staff of the flag into this stump and tried to rally their men around it.

During a lull in the fighting, the Seventy-fifth was able to replenish ammunition in preparation for the next assault. Assault followed repulse followed assault; charges were beaten back with terrible loss of life. The Seventy-fifth knelt behind the logs and held fire until the Confederates were within 50 yards of their line. Then they poured in volume after volume of murderous fire, together with grape

The battle of Chickamauga

and canister from their artillery battery, cutting wide gaps into the Confederate ranks. As many as two-thirds of some units died or were wounded that day.

In late morning, General Rosecrans withdrew his right flank to support his left and was informed that he had a gap in his line. In moving units to shore up the supposed gap, Rosecrans created a yawning, quarter-mile opening in the Union center. Lieutenant General James Longstreet's eight Confederate brigades, five of which had come from Virginia by rail to reinforce Bragg, promptly exploited it, driving one-third of the Union army, including Rosecrans himself, from the field. "The confusion and distress of this rout beggar all description. There were the hurry and tumult of artillery trains, wagons and ambulances rushing to the rear with a sort of orderly confusion, as distressing as panic itself. The Confederates shouting, yelling, running over batteries, wagons and ambulances, rushed on, capturing thousands of prisoners, and killing officers and men."[7] A Federal battery stampeded and ran over a brigade of infantry, injuring many. Ammunition wagons were lost or scattered in the retreat before Longstreet's attack.

The Confederates made it to the rear of the brigade, which changed position to face this foe, ran out of ammunition, then fell back before murderous fire, leaving scores of wounded on the ground.

Both sides in the conflict expended all their ammunition again and again, making it impossible for them to hold the line. When they could, the men grabbed a weapon from their dead or wounded comrades, and when the ammunition did not fit their weapons, threw it away and seized whatever arms they could find. Toward the latter part of the fight, scarcely any order remained, and no defined line. Regiments and companies were inextricably mixed up, and the situation resembled a skirmish on a grand scale rather than the conflict

Cannons fired both grape and canister. Grapeshot were iron balls (usually nine) encased in a fused explosive shell and fired from a cannon. The balls broke apart and scattered on impact. Canister consisted of 27 lead balls sealed in sawdust in a tin casing that scattered when fired from a cannon. They were used primarily in defense of a position.

Lieutenant Albion W. Tourgee, One Hundred Fifth Ohio Infantry: "We moved by the double-quick around a low, wooded knoll, across an open field, faced to the right and advanced in line of battle.... The wave of battle rolled down the line toward us. There seemed to be an interval at our right; we moved by the flank to fill it. It was the worst possible region in which to maneuver an army, being without landmarks or regular slopes, and so thickly wooded that it was impossible to preserve any alignment. Besides, there seemed to be, as we now know there was, an utter lack of fixed and definite plan, and a woeful ignorance of the field. Soldiers are quick to note such things, and one of the Thousand, seeing a group of officers in consultation, said he guessed they were 'pitching pennies' to decide which way the brigade should front ...

"Confusion reigned even before the battle began.... Even the part a single regiment took is almost untraceable."[8]

of a Line of Battle. In some cases units were ordered to advance, bayonets fixed, without any bullets in their rifles.

Horses of the cavalry and artillery that drew the cannon were killed, interfering with troop movement. Woods and fields were set on fire by exploding shells. A cannon ball struck a yellow jacket nest in a tree, causing havoc for the troops below.

As the battle raged around him, Al hurried to help the limping wounded to the field hospitals. Bigger drummers carried stretchers. Al wasn't big enough to move men who were severely wounded, but he could prop up his comrades who were bleeding but still on their feet. He may have helped Private Loren G. King of Company C, who was wounded in his thigh, and Private James Dearinger of Company C, wounded in the mouth. He stepped aside for the hurrying ambulances, aware of how excruciating the jolting of mule-drawn wagons would be to those in serious pain. He flinched below the bursting shells and shrapnel, the hissing bullets. He was vaguely aware of the retreating squads from his overwhelmed brigade, the crash of musketry rolling from the woods in front. If he came upon wounded Confederate soldiers, crying for help, he must have been struck by how vulnerable and innocent they seemed. These broken boys were the enemy? Did he share precious water from his canteen with them? He could have, for surely there was a well with a hand pump at Cloud's house where he could refill it.

"It was a rough-and-tumble, all day long fight, without intrenchments [sic], a series of surprises, of alternating successes, of charges and countercharges, a death grapple of irregular lines in thickets and woods. There was no time for tactics or maneuvering, or counter preparation. . . . a mad, irregular battle very much resembling guerrilla warfare on a vast scale, in which one army was bushwhacking the other, and wherein all the science and art of war went for nothing."[10]

Bayonets: Narrow swords that fastened to the end of a gun barrel for use in hand-to-hand combat.

"The small pond behind the house of widow Eliza Glenn was one of the only water sources available to the fighting Federals. It became known as Bloody Pond because of the injured horses and wounded soldiers who dragged themselves to it and, while drinking, died or stained it with their blood."[9]

The battle of Chickamauga

Wounded soldiers at a field hospital. Treasures of the Civil War from the New-York Historical Society, Digital ID nhnycw/ad ad30058.

During that battle, late on the afternoon of September 20, the field hospitals located at Crawfish Springs and at Cloud's house, to the right and left of the Union lines, fell into the hands of the enemy. Just then Al was helping a wounded comrade, perhaps Private David M. Cox of Company C or Private John McKee of Company G, wounded in the back of his neck, into the field hospital.

A pond on the Chickamauga battlefield. Mathew Brady Photographs of Civil War-Era Personalities and Scenes, National Archives 111-B-5085.

What did he do with his drum while he was helping the wounded? Did he stash it under a tree by the field hospital? In any case, when on the afternoon of September 20 the Confederates overran the field hospital at Cloud's house, Albert Walton—drummer boy of Company C—was made a prisoner, together with some of the badly wounded of the regiment, whom he had helped there. A big, burly Confederate cavalryman smashed Al's drum against a tree. Then he grabbed little Al, observed his youthful appearance, and taunted him in a rough voice, "You ought to be at home, nursing on your mother's breast, instead of here!"[11]

The battle of Chickamauga

In his memoir Al says, "We were deprived of coats, canteens, blankets, caps, and knapsacks. After marching for three miles to the rear of the battle line, stumbling over our gallant dead who had fell for their country and who now lay bleeding, dying upon the field of honor. Never can I forget the ghastly scenes that met my gaze."

Al's military campaign was over. When darkness came, he would not be there with his company to sound Retreat!

Chapter 5 Endnotes

[1] *History*, p. 132.
[2] A good description of the battle is found at <www.ourancestry.com/CivilWarBattles>.
[3] "Personal Recollections of Chickamauga" in *Sketches of War History, 1861-1865: Papers Read before the Ohio Commandery of the Military Order of the Loyal Legion of the United States, 1883-1886*, Vol. I (Wilmington, NC: Broadfoot, 1991, reprint of the 1888 edition).
[4] *History*, p. 143.
[5] *History*, p. 154.
[6] Miller, pp. 144-45.
[7] *History*, p. 169.
[8] *The Story of a Thousand* (Buffalo, NY: S. McGerald & Sons, 1896).
[9] TIME/LIFE, *Voices of the Civil War: Chickamauga*, p. 79.
[10] *History*, p. 151.
[11] *History*, pp. 176-77.

As Longstreet's victorious troops pushed the Federals aside, General George H. Thomas took over command and began consolidating his remaining forces on Horseshoe Ridge and Snodgrass Hill. Although the Confederates launched determined assaults on these forces, they held until after dark. At the end of the day, Thomas knew that, with the rest of the army in flight, he also had to retreat. He sent his hard-pressed units one by one toward McFarland's Gap, melting away in the darkness to Chattanooga, leaving their dead and wounded behind. Confederate field hospitals were too busy to tend to them. Hundreds of blood-covered men lay on the straw-covered ground, untended for days and nights.

Although the Union lost the battle at Chickamauga, they held on to Chattanooga, averting disaster for the Army of the Cumberland.

Of 100,000 men engaged in the two days at Chickamauga, 35,000 of them were dead, wounded, or missing.

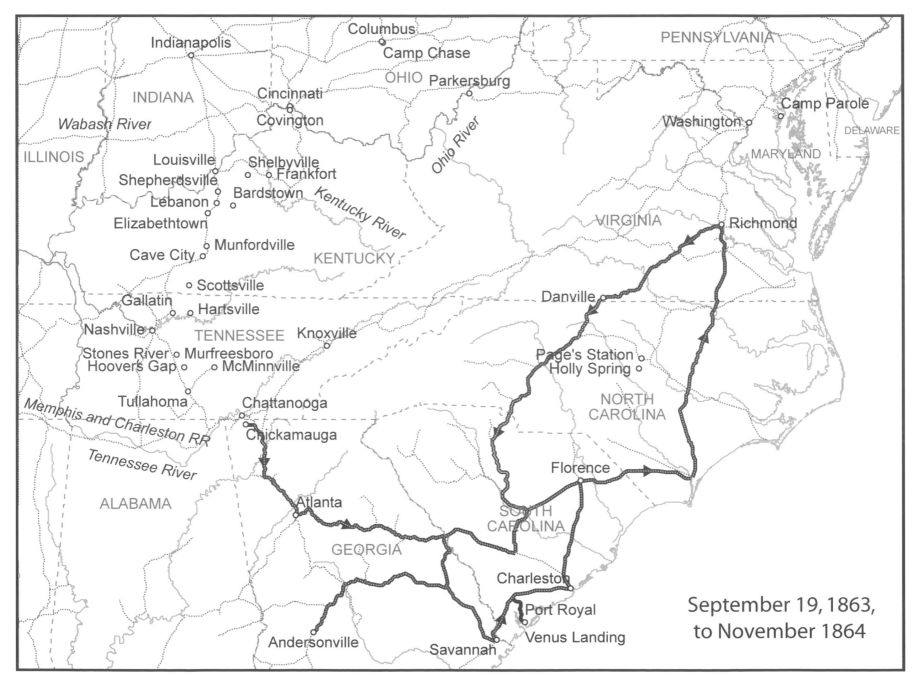

Solid lines show routes that were traveled either on foot or by ship. Lines without arrows indicate routes that Al traveled in both directions.

September 19, 1863,
to November 1864

Prisoner of war

CHAPTER 6 Prisoner of war

Al was astonished. It had never occurred to him that he might become a prisoner of war. Being killed had seemed much more likely.

Seventeen soldiers of the Seventy-fifth had died at Chickamauga;107 were wounded. Of course, officers were not immune to death or capture. Captain William McGinnis, age 45, of Company H, was wounded and captured at Chickamauga. He was first confined in Libby Prison and hospitalized at Richmond, Virginia, with dysentery. He was sent briefly to Andersonville, but as an officer he was soon dispatched to Camp Ogelthorpe at Macon, Georgia, where officers were confined. He died at Savannah, Georgia, in August 1864.

This information comes from the Compiled Military Service Records of Captain McGinnis, Surgeon Arthur, and Surgeon Shaffer.

The two surgeons of the Seventy-fifth working at Cloud's house, Christopher S. Arthur and Abner H. Shaffer, were captured. Arthur was imprisoned at Richmond and paroled. Shaffer was paroled at City Point, Virginia, in November 1863. Paroled prisoners were supposedly sent to Northern camps, but many soldiers simply went home or returned to their units. Confederate prisoners were required to take an oath of allegiance to the Union before they were released.

When Federal soldiers were captured by the Confederates, they disappeared into historical limbo, for many Confederate records did not survive the war. Union (as well as many Confederate) records are in the National Archives. Each company in the Seventy-fifth and every other regiment had a clerk appointed to keep what were called "Regimental Books." These were prepared daily and included detailed information about every soldier as well as morning reports that accounted for the presence or absence of every soldier in a company. After the war the company reports covering all the companies of the regiment were bound into large ledgers.

Morning Report for September 1863. Regimental Books, National Archives Record Group 94, Entries 112 - 115.

On September 19 and 20, 1863, the clerk of Company C entered "Battle of Chickamauga, Ga." On September 21 he wrote "H. H. Rayburn, J. Whistler, James Quinn, James Thorington, Albert Walton, David Cox. Missing in action."

On the muster rolls, captured soldiers were simply marked "absent" or "absent without leave" or "missing in action." It was only when soldiers were paroled or exchanged that Union records could be updated with information provided by the returning soldiers. There was a Commissary General of Prisoners, who maintained volumes of "Exchanged Prisoners of War, 1861-1865." Al's name appears in these. Eventually a "Memorandum from Prisoner of War Records" was filled out with whatever information had been gathered. It was filed in each soldier's Compiled Military Service Record.

Prisoners of war awaiting transportation. Mathew Brady Photographs of Civil War-Era Personalities and Scenes, National Archives 111-B-3482.

R	75	**Ind.**

Hayden H. Rayburn,

5ᵗ Cook, Co. C , 75 Reg't Indiana Infantry.

Appears on

Company Descriptive Book

of the organization named above.

DESCRIPTION.

Age *18* years; height *5* feet *4* inches.

Complexion *Light*

Eyes *Blue* ; hair *Brown*

Where born *Lawrence, Ind.*

Occupation *Tinner,*

ENLISTMENT.

When *July 9* , 1862

Where *Kokomo,*

By whom *F.M. Bryant* ; term *3* y'rs.

Remarks: *Wounded at the battle of Chicka-mauga Sept. 19/63, & a prisoner. Discharged June 27/64, Surg'ᵗ Certificate of Disability from gun-shot wound at Chickamauga Sept. 19/63.*

Hinsley

(883g) Copyist.

W	75	**Ind.**

Samuel B. Weaver,

, Co. C , 75 Reg't Indiana Infantry.

Appears on

Company Descriptive Book

of the organization named above.

DESCRIPTION.

Age *18* years; height *6* feet — inches.

Complexion *Light*

Eyes *Blue* ; hair *Dark*

Where born *Clark, Ohio,*

Occupation *Farmer,*

ENLISTMENT.

When *July 16* , 1862,

Where *Kokomo,*

By whom *F.M. Bryant* ; term *3* y'rs.

Remarks: *Wounded at the Battle of Chickamauga Sept 20/63,*

Hinsley

(883g) Copyist.

W	75	**Ind.**

John B. Whistler,

, Co. C , 75 Reg't Indiana Infantry.

Appears on

Company Descriptive Book

of the organization named above.

DESCRIPTION.

Age *20* years; height *5* feet *8* inches.

Complexion *Dark*

Eyes *Blue* ; hair *Dark*

Where born *Piqua, Ohio,*

Occupation *Farmer,*

ENLISTMENT.

When *July 18* , 1862

Where *Kokomo,*

By whom *F.M. Bryant* ; term *3* y'rs.

Remarks: *Wounded & a prisoner at the Battle of Chickamauga Sept. 19/63. Had leg amputated at Atlanta, Ga,*

Hinsley

(883g) Copyist.

Q	75	**Ind.**

James R. Quinn,

, Co. C , 75 Reg't Indiana Infantry.

Appears on

Company Descriptive Book

of the organization named above.

DESCRIPTION.

Age *20* years; height *5* feet *6* inches.

Complexion *Light*

Eyes *Hazel* ; hair *Blk.*

Where born *City New York,*

Occupation *Farmer,*

ENLISTMENT.

When *July 8* , 1862,

Where *Kokomo,*

By whom *F.M. Bryant* ; term *3* y'rs.

Remarks: *Wounded at the Battle of Chickamauga Sept. 19/63. Promoted to Corp. Aug. 1863,*

Hinsley

(883g) Copyist.

Private Hayden H. Rayburn, age 18, of Company C was wounded at Chickamauga, taken to the Crawfish Springs hospital, and transferred to the hospital in Annapolis on September 28. He was discharged June 29, 1864, as sergeant.

Private Samuel B. Weaver, age 18, also of Company C, was wounded in the foot, taken to Crawfish Springs field hospital, and mustered out.

Private John B. Whistler, age 20, was wounded and sent to hospital in Atlanta, where his leg was amputated and he died on November 1, 1863.

Corporal James Quinn, age 20, was wounded September 20 and was also taken to Crawfish Springs. He was paroled from Nashville, Tennessee, in February 1864.

Taken from Compiled Military Service Records, National Archives

Prisoner of war

The Federal prisoners taken at Chickamauga must have been held in an enclosure somewhere on the battlefield. They would have looked among the crowd for men from their own regiment, the only bond they had with each other. Al found Private David Cox, age 27, and Private James C. Thorington, age 31, both badly injured, and John B. Whistler, age 20, all three of his own Company C, among the prisoners. Surgeon Arthur was also in the group. They were held until September 29, then bundled into boxcars and sent to Richmond along with the following men from the Seventy-fifth Indiana Volunteers:[1]

- Sergeant John Rhine, Company K
- Private Jeremiah Sherman, Company I
- Private John C. Malsby, Company D, who died in Libby Prison
- Private Silas Moorehead, Company A, who was hospitalized in Richmond

The following men may also have been sent to Richmond, but the date of their transfer is unknown:

- Sergeant Wesley King, Company B, who was hospitalized in Richmond
- Private John D. McKee, Company G
- Private William A. Lawson, Company A (brother of James)
- Private James M. Lawson, Company A (brother of William)
- Private Byron Kurtz, Company I
- Private John N. Wilson, Company G
- Private Samuel Landers, Company I, who died in Richmond
- Private Daniel Wilcoxen, Company K

Years later Al told his children that he helped a wounded officer in the days after the field hospital at Chickamauga was captured. I like to think that the officer Al helped was Sergeant Wesley King, whose left hand was wounded at Chickamauga. He would have needed help climbing into a boxcar, buttoning his pants buttons (no zippers in those days), and competing for rations. I hope that Al had been able to snatch up his haversack from under the tree where he was captured, that he had some of his week's rations still stashed away in it, and that he shared them with Sergeant King.

I realize that my grandfather's "officer" could have been from a different regiment, for the field hospital would have treated the wounded from all the regiments fighting at Chickamauga, not just the Indiana Brigade. Many regiments from other states were in General Rosecrans's field army.

Looking through a number of service records, I have found that soldiers who were captured at the Crawfish Springs field hospital at Chickamauga were soon paroled. Taking prisoners was not always convenient, for someone had to guard them and move them off the battlefield and care for those who were sick or wounded. If no prison was available, if the soldiers holding the captives were needed urgently elsewhere, or if the doctors were too busy with their own wounded to care for enemy soldiers, it was simpler to parole captives than to waste manpower guarding them. Al, unfortunately, was not one of the lucky ones to be paroled.

I wish I had listened more carefully to my father's stories. I've searched the rolls of the Seventy-fifth for a likely candidate whom my grandfather might have helped and then checked the military service records. When you consider that a total of three million service records were kept during the Civil War, it's not surprising that they are not all complete, nor that some may have contained errors. Private James Dearinger of Company C, who was wounded at Missionary Ridge, has his name spelled three different ways in his military service record: Dearinger, Daringer, and Darringer.

I also try to picture how David Bittle Floyd went about writing the history of the Seventy-fifth Indiana Infantry Volunteers Regiment. Compiled Military Service Records were not available to him. He must have written many letters, asking for information. He surely attended annual state reunions of the Grand Army of the Republic and gathered individual information on those occasions. The *History* was not published until 1893, so obviously it was a work of many years' duration. Remember that he wrote it all in longhand. Typewriters were not invented until 1874.

Chapter 6 Endnotes

[1] Information about each individual soldier was found in his Compiled Military Service Record, National Archives. The Compiled Military Service Record consists of information taken primarily from muster rolls, returns, and pay vouchers.

Prisoner of war

CHAPTER 7   Richmond Prison

Almon wrote in his memoir that "There were five hundred of us captured at the same time and we were packed in a dismal old blacksmith shop surrounded by strong rebel guards. There were so many of us packed in this shop that there seemed hardly standing room and to sleep seemed impossible to me. I could not help thinking of home. How my heart yearned for my dear old friends Arland Kelly and Jacob Lair, and then came the awful thought that they too might be among the piles of dead on the battlefield. At early dawn the next morning we started out for Dalton and arriving there were packed into freight cars bound for Atlanta. Upon arrival there we were placed in a pen enclosed by a stockade. We remained there a few days, then boxed in freight cars again, we started for Richmond, Va., and were thrown into a tobacco warehouse nearly opposite Libby Prison. Here we were fed twice a day, but not nearly to satisfy our hunger."

Libby Prison in Richmond[1] consisted of three tenement (loft-style) buildings, each four stories high. Built between 1845 and 1852, they were intended for use in the tobacco industry. The three buildings, designated east, middle, and west, were connected by inner doors.

The west building was leased by Captain Luther Libby, a ship chandler from Maine, who put up a sign: L. LIBBY & SON, SHIP CHANDLERS. Because so many federal prisoners were being sent to Richmond, these buildings were commandeered for prisoner and hospital use. The buildings were converted to their new use so rapidly that Captain Libby's sign was never taken down—hence the name Libby Prison.

Prisoners were held on the upper floors. The west ground floor was used for offices and guard-rooms, the middle as a kitchen. Each floor had a water closet that became a privy and polluted the air of the entire building. The cellars contained cells for dangerous prisoners, spies, slaves under death sentence, and a carpenter shop.

John McElroy wrote a book about his experiences in prison in Richmond, Andersonville, and Florence.[2] He was not of Al's regiment, but rather from Company L of the Sixteenth Illinois Cavalry. His first-person accounts show what prison life was like. For example, "The room in which we were was barely large enough for all of us to lie down at once. Even then it required pretty close 'spooning' together—so close in fact that all sleeping along one side would have to turn at once. It was funny to watch this operation. All, for instance, would be lying on their right sides. They would begin to get tired, and one of the wearied ones would sing out to the Sergeant who was in command of the row, 'Sergeant, let's spoon the other way!' That individual would reply, 'All right. Attention! Left Spoon!!' and the whole line would at once flop over on their left sides."[3]

Libby Prison in Richmond, Virginia, beside the James River. Photo by Alexander Gardner, Civil War glass plate negative collection, Library of Congress LC-DIG-cwpb-01253.

Richmond Prison

"The Winter days passed on, one by one . . .. The rations kept growing lighter and lighter; the quantity of bread remained the same, but the meat diminished, and occasionally days would pass without any being issued. Then we received a pint or less of soup made from beans or peas . . . but this, too, suffered continued changes, in the gradually increasing proportion of James River water, and decreasing of that of beans."[4] McElroy also mentions that the beans and peas were all infested with weevils so that the soup was full of bugs. He was hungry enough to eat bugs without protest.

"I had come into prison, as did most other prisoners, absolutely destitute of dishes or cooking utensils. The well-used, half-canteen frying pan, the blackened quart cup, and the spoon, which had formed the usual kitchen outfit of the cavalryman in the field, were in the haversack on my saddle, and were lost to me when I was separated from my horse. Now, when we were told we were to draw soup, I was in great danger of losing my ration from having no vessel in which to receive it. There were but a few tin cups in prison, and these were, of course, wanted by their owners. By great good fortune I found an empty fruit can, holding about a quart. I was also lucky enough to find a piece of wire from which to make a bail. I next manufactured a spoon and knife combined from a bit of hoop-iron."[5]

The prisoners cooked their inadequate rations with inadequate fuel. Al tried to look after Sergeant King, making space for him among the men crowded into the upper floor and bringing food when it was available. He doubtless had the same problems as John McElroy when it came to the need for eating utensils.

On November 26 Sergeant King was sent to the hospital with pneumonia. He had been kind to Al, who worried that he might never see him again. At age 32 Sergeant King might have very much resembled the father Al had lost when he was five years old, and he had become very attached to the older man.

Al wrote in his memoir that "David Cox of my own company was my bunkmate here. He being sick when captured, his condition now seemed worse, and despite my efforts to revive him, he left this earthly home of pain and woe and reached a brighter land." James Thorington of Company C died in Richmond as well. Their bodies were removed without Al ever knowing what happened to them.

"The nights grew extremely cold and we were forced to sleep on bare floors without blankets or pillows. We often got up at night and run around in order to keep warm and also to chew tobacco stems to keep from starving. The vermin increased despite efforts to keep clean. We were obliged to wear the same clothing while in captivity and had neither soap or water."

Private Samuel Sanders of Company I, Seventy-fifth Indiana Volunteers, who was captured December 19, 1863, near Shallow Ford, Tennessee, died on March 5, 1864, while a prisoner of war at Richmond.

More than 50,000 Federal soldiers passed through Libby Prison or one of the other prisons in Richmond while the Confederacy fought its war. The large number of Union prisoners confined in Richmond seemed a threat in the Confederate capital. That and a food shortage led Confederate officials to look for a place that could provide greater security and a more abundant food supply.

Chapter 7 Endnotes

[1] This information comes from a web site: <www.censusdiggins.com/prison_libby.html>
[2] John McElroy, *Andersonville, a Story of Rebel Military Prisons, Fifteen Months a Guest of the So-called Southern Confederacy* (Toledo, OH: D.R. Locke, 1879).
[3] McElroy, p. 104.
[4] McElroy, p. 101.
[5] McElroy, p. 102.

CHAPTER 8   Danville Prison

On December 12, 1863,[1] Al was sent to Danville. He wrote that "the rebel officers appeared in our prison and ordered us to stand in line, telling us as they counted us off, that we were going to be exchanged the following day. Oh how delighted we leaped with joy at this good news. That same night, two of our boys approached the window to look out and were instantly killed. There lay two who just a moment before had wept for joy at the thought of seeing home and loved ones again, but there they lay in innocent sleep never to return to their earthly home.

"At last the joyful morning dawned and we were looking forward with great pleasure to the hour when we could see home once more. Early in the morning the rebel chieftan [*sic*] Ross entered the prison and formed us in line, gave us each a whole loaf of bread, then marched us down the stairs to the street. Upon looking up to the windows of Libby Prison, I noticed a number of our officers and among them I discovered my regimental surgeon, Dr. C. S. Arthur. I waved my hand to him as I did not dare to speak, and he recognized me by smiling.[2]

"We soon arrived at Richmond railroad depot and here were crowded into Cattle cars and rode one hundred and fifty miles to Danville, VA. Guards were stationed inside and on top of the car, prepared to shoot any man that threatened to escape. Three of our boys tried to escape by jumping out of the car window, but were unsuccessful. One of them was instantly killed, another wounded so badly that he died, and the other was captured and brought back to the train and punished."

Danville is located 143 miles southwest of Richmond and four miles north of the North Carolina border. It was a safe distance from Union attack and had good railroad connections. Provisions there would be cheaper. Several of the warehouses there had already been converted into military hospitals. It could relieve overcrowding in Richmond prisons.

Danville Prison[3] was not one prison camp, but six vacant brick buildings, mostly tobacco and cotton warehouses, in the center of town. One of the buildings had an attached bakehouse and cooking range with the capability of preparing rations for 3,000 men. There were three other warehouses, all within 100 yards of each other, that had the combined capacity to hold 2,300 prisoners. Not far away, two additional buildings, with a capacity of almost 1,300, came into use. The structures were stripped of all furnishings, including chairs and lamps.

These buildings were three stories plus attics, with rows of large wooden support posts running down the middle. Each floor had a wide open area of about 2,400 square feet. Prisoners were confined on the upper two floors, while the lower floor was patrolled by guards. Wooden staircases along the walls connected the floors.

Prisoners found themselves with a mere six feet by two feet of bare, hard floor. They lay in long rows, two rows with their heads to the side walls and two with their heads toward the center of the room, with narrow aisles between the rows of feet. A single pot-bellied stove was installed on each floor of the building and gave off noxious fumes.

With Al at Danville were two privates from Company A, brothers James M. (age 24) and William A. Lawson (age 21); Sergeant Wesley King (age 32) of Company B; two privates from Company G, John D. McKee (age 24) and John N. Wilson (age 28); two privates from Company I, Byron Kurtz (age 19) and Jeremiah Sherman (age 23); and one private from Company K, Daniel Wilcoxen (age 28). These men may not have known each other before, but the fact that they were from the same regiment would have drawn them together while they were incarcerated at Richmond.

They had almost no clothing and no blankets. Soldiers marching into battle did not carry their knapsacks in which they stored their blanket, extra clothes, eating

Danville Prison

The prison at Danville occupied four warehouses. Illustration by J.M. Thurston, Company F, Ninetieth Ohio Infantry, Library of Congress LC-USZ62-15630.

utensils, etc. They left these on the wagons behind the combat zone. They did carry their haversacks, containing rations, and their water canteens, for they would need to drink during any lull in the battle.

When the pitiful food rations were dumped on the filthy floor at Danville, Al was small enough to wiggle his way through the men fighting for their share. He grabbed chunks of cornbread for himself and for Sergeant King, who was still weak from the pneumonia he had suffered in Richmond. Al stayed close to him where he was propped against a wall, making sure he was included in his latrine group so that he could help the sergeant with the buttons on his pants.

They whittled the wooden supports and rafters of the rooms to the breaking point to obtain slivers of wood which they boiled to make "coffee." They attempted to ignore rat dung in the rice, pea bugs in the peas, and worms in the cabbage soup, which was diluted with pails of water from the Dan River. After several attempted escapes, prisoners were no longer allowed access to the ground floor or yards. Six prisoners at a time were escorted to the latrines under heavy guard. The men with diarrhea were humiliated by restricted latrine privileges. The smell was nauseating.

Only limited amounts of firewood were available for heat in a cold winter, but many of the prisoners had no coat or blanket and, like Al, only one shirt, which they were never able to wash. Can you picture him, shivering, huddled over that one shirt, stiff with Private Kidder's blood, picking the lice from it?

Daily rations usually consisted of coarse, half-baked cornbread (made of corn and husk and cob all ground together), peas, cabbage soup, and maybe some salted fish. Some prisoners actually boiled or stewed rats into soup. Lack of nutrients led to scurvy. Men who had weighed 200 pounds when they were captured often weighed half that when they were released.

The confined space in the sometimes stifling warehouses allowed for the rampant spread of disease. Smallpox broke out in Richmond prisons and spread quickly to Danville. The Union blockade of the Southern coastline had all but stopped the flow of provisions and medicine into the Confederacy, and there was little the doctors could do to help the desperately ill prisoners. When smallpox subsided, chronic diarrhea became the prevalent cause of death. More than 1,300 Union soldiers died at Danville from illness and malnutrition, among them Private John D. McKee of Company G and Private James M. Lawson of Company A (who succumbed to smallpox on Christmas Day).

Danville Prison

Al never forgot an act of kindness at Danville: "One morning a pleasant-faced Confederate officer entered the prison and ordered those who suffered from small pox to be removed from among us. Seeing me kneeling beside one of my dying comrades he gave me a pleasant smile and said 'Why, little one, you are indeed a small soldier, and if you promise me that you will not run away, I will put you with some of your own men in the bakery.' Then giving orders to the guards, he took me by the hand and bade me to follow him. He told me his name was Major Moffatt and then asked my name and where I lived. Passing his arm through mine, he asked the reason that my blouse was so stiff and hard. I told him it was the blood of one of my wounded comrades. We became fast friends; he often invited me to his office and was always kind and loving and this was the only gleam of sunshine in my prison life."

The Confederate prison facilities were completely inadequate, so Al and Sergeant King and their buddies stayed at Danville until the prison at Andersonville was opened. They may have been joined at some point by Private William Evans, age 22, wounded in his hip at Chickamauga, and Private Samuel Bock, age 20, both from Company I and both captured on a scouting expedition near Shallow Ford, Tennessee, on December 19, 1863.

CHAPTER 8 ENDNOTES

[1] According to a "Memorandum from Prisoner of War Records" in Al's Compiled Military Service Record.
[2] Al wrote that "In 1895 I met Dr. Arthur at a regimental reunion held at Warren, Indiana, and we recalled all the little incidents that happened when he and I were together."
[3] An excellent article on the web by Patricia B. Mitchell gives a detailed description of Danville Prison. <www.victorianvilla.com/sims-mithcell/local/articles/phsp/008/>.

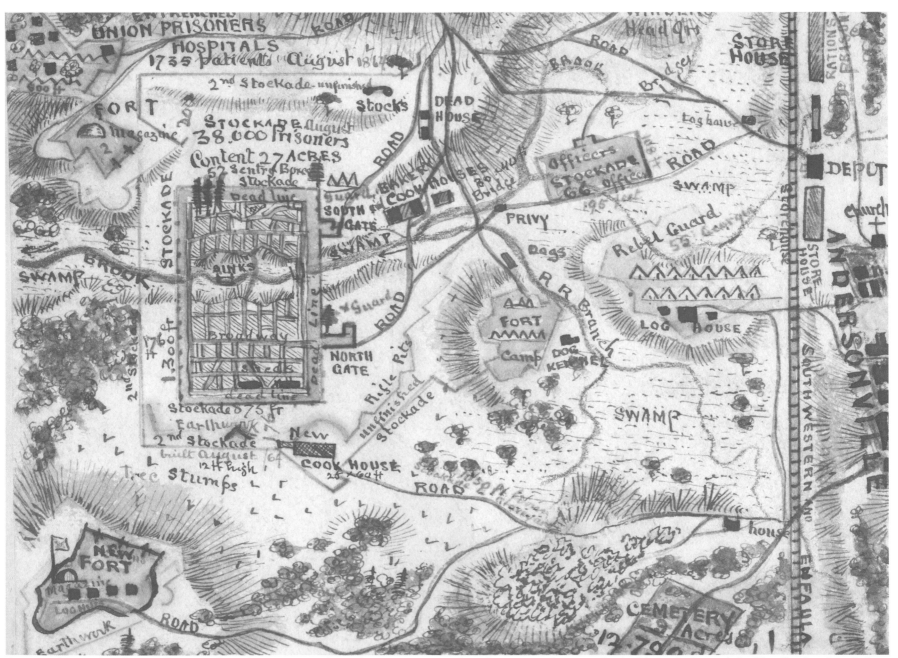

Section of map of Andersonville Prison by Robert Knox Sneden, who was a prisoner there for six months. Note the double stockades and the "deadline" within. Robert Sneden's scrapbook is part of the collections of the Virginia Historical Society.

Andersonville Stockade

CHAPTER 9   Andersonville Stockade

Soldiers of both sides suffered in prison camps North and South, but Andersonville, in the piney woods of central Georgia, was the worst of a horrible lot. Although it existed for barely a year, about 45,000 captured Union troops were sent there, and of these nearly 13,000 died of disease, malnutrition, and exposure to the elements.

Work building the stockade began under the direction of Captain W. Sidney Winder in January 1864, but the men who were needed to do the work had to be forced to do it. Supplies, tools, and equipment were hard to find. The plan to construct barracks was abandoned because lumber was snapped up by the railroads at high prices. Able-bodied men refused to drive the cattle needed for meat; mills were too busy to grind corn for food for prisoners.

While he was attempting to equip the prison, Captain Winder received word that the prisoners in Richmond were to be removed to Andersonville at the rate of 400 a day. The first detachment left Richmond February 18, 1864, and arrived at the new prison February 27. They followed a zigzag route because they were sent by train.

John McElroy also made that journey: "Packed closely in old, dilapidated stock and box cars, as if cattle in shipment to market, we pounded along slowly, and apparently interminably . . . . The railroads of the South were already in very bad condition, . . . as nearly ruined as they could well be and still run."[1] "For four or five days the decrepit little locomotive strained along, dragging after it the rattling old cars. The scenery . . . was a flat, almost unending stretch of pine barrens . . . ."[2]

An enormous amount of text has been written about Andersonville Prison. As a primary source for this chapter I read a long, hand-written document by a Confederate surgeon, assuming he would be an unbiased observer. His report was entitled "Observations upon the Disease of the Federal Prisoners confined in Camp Sumpter [sic] Andersonville, in Sumpter County, Georgia, instituted with a view to illustrate chiefly the Origins & Causes of Hospital Gangrene, the Relations of Continued & Malarial Fevers, and the Pathology of Camp Diarrhoea [sic] & Dysentery" by Joseph Jones, Surgeon, P. & C. S., Professor of Medicine (Chemistry) in the Medical College of Georgia, at Augusta, Georgia. This document contains an unvarnished description of conditions at Andersonville and confirms the recollections of my grandfather and of John McElroy.[3]

"About midnight the train stopped, and we were ordered off. We were in the midst of a forest of tall trees that loaded the air with the heavy balsamic odor peculiar to pine trees. . . . Stretched out into the darkness was a double row of great heaps of burning pitch pine that smoked and flamed fiercely, and lit up a little space around in the somber forest with a ruddy glare. Between these two rows lay a road, which we were ordered to take.

"Five hundred weary men moved slowly through double lines of guards. Five hundred men marched silently toward the gates that were to shut out life and hope from most of them forever. A quarter of a mile from the railroad we came to a massive palisade of great squared logs standing upright in the ground. The fires blazed up and showed us a section of these, and two massive wooden gates with heavy iron hinges and bolts. They swung open as we stood there and we passed into the great space beyond.

"We were in Andersonville."[4]

Because there are few surviving Confederate records, we have no specific dates for when the many soldiers arrived at Andersonville. Al was sent from Danville to Andersonville shortly after it opened in February 1864. In his memoir Al wrote, "We journeyed in flat cars through rain and sunshine until we reached our destination and then marched over the burning sands to the prison where nothing but starvation and brutality existed. Upon our arrival at the prison, an officer stepped to the front and assumed command. We were soon informed that this was Captain Henry Wirz. He walked along our line counting, and as one of our boys was a little out of line with his shoulders, being so sick that he could hardly stand up, Wirz, after cursing him a while, took out his revolver and placed the muzzle against his forehead and discharged it. Our dear comrade sank prostrate upon the sands, to rise no more. This was our first introduction to this brutal fiend who was to have charge of all of us.

"Capt. Wirz was a very quick tempered man. I saw him murder two men. One was a negro soldier with a running sore on his jaw caused by a wound he had received

Andersonville Stockade

A new batch of prisoners arrives at Andersonville. Pencil drawing by William Waud, Morgan collection of Civil War drawings, Library of Congress LC-DIG-ppmsca-21764.

Drummer Boy of Company C

Andersonville Prison as seen by John L. Ransom, author and publisher of "Andersonville Story, Escape and List of the Dead." The three stockades are clearly visible, as is the stream running across the middle of the inner stockade. Library of Congress LC-DIG-pga-02585.

Andersonville Stockade

in battle. Wirz set him to digging a well. He was not able to do it, and as he did not work very fast, he was whipped until he died of exhaustion. The other man escaped through a tunnel from the stockade and ran into a swamp and lay in the mud to keep away from the hounds until the owner of the hounds came and set the dogs on him. The poor man, badly bitten and also bleeding, was taken to Capt. Wirz, who pounded him on the head until dead."

Al described the camp: "The prison covered fifteen acres of ground enclosed by a high stockade of hewed pine logs, twelve feet above ground and six beneath; closely guarded by numerous sentinels who stood in elevated boxes overlooking the camp. In the center of the camp was a swamp occupying three or four acres. Along the edge of the swamp from one side of the camp to the other ran a little shallow brook, three

Andersonville Stockade, summer of 1864. Note the sentry boxes. Library of Congress LC-USZ62-198.

or four feet wide. This, with a few small springs, furnished the water. No shelter was provided to us by the Rebels. We were exposed to the scorching rays of the sun and the pouring rain. The horrors of Andersonville are beyond description or imagination. The dead-line was a slender railing all around the inside of the stockade and about a rod from it. The men who crossed over or under this, whether ignorantly done or not, met with instant death from the vigilant sentinels."

Several other men of the Seventy-fifth Indiana Infantry went to Andersonville. Their Compiled Military Service Records tell their stories:

- Sergeant Wesley King was by then 33 years old, 5 feet 7 inches tall, with light complexion, auburn hair, and dark eyes. He had been a mechanic.
- Sergeant John Rhine was 31, 5 feet 11 inches tall, with light complexion, hazel eyes, and brown hair. He came from an Indiana farm.
- Private Jeremiah Sherman was 24, 6 feet tall, with dark complexion, blue eyes, and dark hair. He had also been a farmer.
- Private William A. Lawson was 22, 6 feet 1 inch tall, with light complexion, blue eyes, and light hair. He had been a farmer. His brother James had died at Danville.
- Private John N. Wilson was 29, 5 feet 8 and 3/4 inches tall, with sandy complexion, blue eyes, and light hair. He had been a farmer.
- Private Byron Kurtz was 20, with light complexion, blue eyes, and light hair. He had been a farmer.
- Private Edmund H. Brown was 31, 5 feet 8 inches tall, with light complexion, blue eyes, and dark hair. He had been a carpenter.
- Private Samuel Bock was 21, with dark complexion, black eyes, and black hair. He had been a farmer.
- First Lieutenant William McGinnis was 47, 5 feet tall, with dark complexion, hazel eyes, and black hair. He had been a mechanic/blacksmith.

These men may not all have come from Danville together. But they sought each other out at Andersonville and stayed together, as did men from every military unit, because there was comfort in familiar faces and a shared military history. The group they formed was called a mess, that is, a place where soldiers eat their meals, because they received their meager rations in mess units.

The first priority on their arrival was to build some kind of shelter from the Georgia sun and weather. The logs for the stockade had been cut from inside the enclosure, leaving no trees to provide shade for the prisoners. Al scrounged for any bits of lumber and branches remaining from the building of the stockade. He wrote that "my bunkmates dug a hole in the ground with a half a canteen for a shovel and

The gate at Andersonville Stockade. Note the sentries in their boxes. Drawing by T. Miller, Morgan collection of Civil War drawings, Library of Congress LC-DIG-ppmsca-22821.

an old case knife for a pick, and this hole was used as a shelter at night. This was similar to the life of a groundhog or a woodchuck. No language can express the suffering endured by those who entered prisons."

In John McElroy's account, "Nothing showed the inborn capacity of the Northern soldier to take care of himself better than the way in which we accomplished this [shelter] with the rude materials at our command. No ax, spade nor matlock [*sic*] was allowed us by the Rebels . . . The only tools were pocket knives . . . . Yet, despite all these drawbacks, we had quite a village of huts erected in a few days, ... The withes and poles that grew in the swamp were bent into the shape of the semi-circular bows that support the canvas covers of army wagons, and both ends thrust into the ground. . . . They were held in place by weaving, basket-wise, a network of briers and vines. Tufts of the long leaves that are the distinguishing characteristic of the Georgia pine . . . were wrought into this network until a thatch was formed, that was a fair protection against the rain . . .."[5]

Al soon realized that the prisoners who arrived first and were able to build huts were much better off than later arrivals. They could keep almost dry when it rained, and when summer came they had some protection from the heartless sun. He pitied those who had no tents, for they sat or lay exposed on the hill-side both day and night.

John McElroy wrote, "No wood was issued to us. The only way of getting it was to stand around the gate for hours until a guard off duty could be coaxed or hired to accompany a small party to the woods, to bring back a load of such knots and limbs as could be picked up. Our chief persuaders to the guards to do us this favor were rings, pencils, knives, combs, and such trifles as we might have in our pockets, and more especially, the brass buttons on our uniforms. . . . Our regular fee for an

Another prisoner of war at Andersonville recorded his experiences there. Private Robert Knox Sneden of the Fortieth New York Volunteers of Mozart Regiment was captured during a night raid in November 1863 at Brandy Station, Virginia. He arrived at Andersonville on February 28, 1864.

He wrote of the misery caused by rain: "The rain beat down thousands of shelters and shanties flat to the ground. Those who were in burrows or in any kind of sunken tent had to be pulled out by their comrades to prevent drowning as every hole was full of rain water in ten minutes time. In the streets leading to the swamp, which were now good sized brooks, were floating down the hill clothing, pans, hats and caps, shoes, and any and everything which had been in the tents. All were scrambling to recover these, yelling and swearing—while the wind blew everything flat and the crashing of thunder was terrific."[7]

After another storm: "Cold and wet. Everyone drenched through and the mud soon made in the camp several inches thick. I, with hundreds of others sat up all night bailing out our shanties and trying to stop the leaks in the rotten blankets which served us for roofs. Those who lived in holes were drowned out and the sick men had to be pulled out of them by their comrades."[8]

Andersonville Stockade

escort for three of us to the woods was six over-coat or dress-coat buttons, or ten or twelve jacket buttons. All in the mess contributed to this fund, and the fuel obtained was carefully guarded and husbanded."[6]

Some of the soldiers brought into the stockade had money in their pockets, leading to a thriving trade in wood (three tent poles cost $10), beans, molasses, onions, and whiskey made of sorghum. One greenback was worth seven or eight Confederate dollars, and the guards coveted the Federal currency.

Prisoners inside Andersonville Stockade. The wagon in the center may contain bags of cornmeal. Based on photo by A.J. Riddle. Treasures of the Civil War from the New-York Historical Society, Digital ID nhnycw/aa aa02056.

John McElroy described their frustration: "Never, during my whole prison life, did I see so much as a tin cup or a bucket issued to a prisoner. Starving men were driven to all sorts of shifts for want of these. Pantaloons or coats were pulled off and their sleeves or legs used to draw a mess's meal in. Boots were common vessels for carrying water, and when the feet of these gave way, the legs were ingeniously closed up with pine pegs, so as to form rude leathern buckets. Men whose pocket knives had escaped the search at the gates made very ingenious little tubs and buckets, and these enabled us to get along after a fashion."[9]

Private Sneden wrote that "iron skillets were issued to us by the Rebels [on March 3, 1864] to bake bread in. One was given to every mess of fifty men. . . . it was so much in demand that we would have to wait until midnight for it."[10]

When Al was scraping their meager ration of dried beans into his cap, did he notice that all the guards had grey beards? Did he ask Sergeant King, "Why are all the guards old men?"

"The able-bodied men of Georgia are all in the army. The state has to recruit men too old to fight to do guard duty."

If Al thought about this for a while, he might have said, "But there are so many of us. Couldn't we overpower them?"

"You'd think so. But that's what the 'deadline' is for. If you cross into that forbidden space along the stockade, you'll be shot by one of the sentries at the top of the stockade without any questions asked beforehand."

Al knew this. He had seen men deliberately walk into that space in order to end the misery they were suffering. Sergeant King might have asked, "What would you do if you did breach the deadline? You couldn't climb the stockade. I doubt if even masses of men could push it over. And all the time the guards would be shooting nonstop."

Al thought about the hopelessness of the situation for a long time before he conceded the futility of fighting back. He watched men digging caves, a daily effort as

Prisoner is shot by a guard while taking part of the deadline for firewood. Illustration by Robert Knox Sneden who kept a diary while a prisoner at Andersonville. Part of the collections of the Virginia Historical Society.

they tried to shelter from the elements. Some of them were also digging tunnels, and Al had a brief moment of hope when he saw this. But frequently the tunnel-diggers were betrayed by someone seeking favor with the guards. Even if they escaped beyond the double stockade, they were hunted down by dogs and brought back inside, torn and bleeding.

Drummer Boy of Company C

Al wrote, "Rebel speakers entered the prison and told us that the Union was being badly whipped and tried to persuade us to join their army. Union prisoners now arrived from Atlanta, and we huddled about them, listening to their stories, which was vastly different from what the Rebel speakers had told us. I discovered from among them two faces from my own regiment, William Smith [from Company F] and [James] Binegar [from Company A]."

Boredom followed them from Danville. The hours dragged slowly with nothing to do except grumble and wait or dream of exchange or escape. Imagine spending several months on one tiny patch of ground with nothing to pass the time—no letters, no reading material, nothing to whittle, no room to play ball if anyone had a ball, no escape from the broiling sun, the rain, the dirt and vermin and mosquitoes, with sickness creeping everywhere. Killing lice became a game to pass the tedious time. Some of the men set quotas, resolving to kill three hundred lice every day.

As the weather grew warmer and the number of prisoners increased, Al found the lice increasing rapidly in numbers. They lived in the hot sand under his feet; steams of them climbed up his legs like ants swarming up a tree.

John McElroy wrote, "To be compelled to lie around in vacuous idleness—to spend days that should be crowded full of action in a monotonous routine of hunting lice, gathering at roll-call, and drawing and cooking our scanty rations, was torturing."[11]

Al looked at the chaos around him, at the complete loss of dignity that inhumane conditions imposed on his fellow prisoners, and wondered how they could ever be redeemed. Let's assume that Sergeant King encouraged Al to talk about his apprehensions. Eventually he told him about his father. Young as he had been when his father died, Al remembered bushy eyebrows and riding on his father's foot to a song about Banbury Cross and "a fine lady upon a white horse." When he told

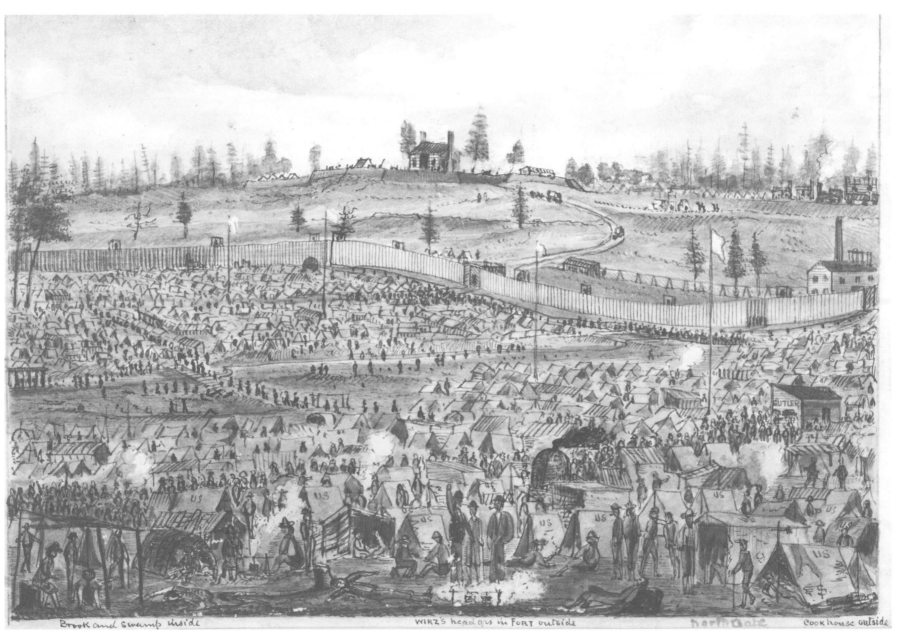

Brook and swamp inside   WIRZ'S head qrs in FORT outside   North Gate   Cookhouse outside

View of the interior of Andersonville prison, showing Wirz's headquarters at the top. Note the cookhouse on the right center where Al may have worked, enabling him to leave the stockade for brief periods and perhaps providing him with extra rations. Watercolor taken from Robert Knox Sneden's diary, part of the Virginia Historical Society's collections.

Drummer Boy of Company C   101

Sergeant King about his vicious stepfather, the older man understood the needs of a fatherless boy, and listened attentively to his anguish.

When the other men from the Seventy-fifth gathered around, they discussed their reasons for joining the army and what they had learned from the experience. If Al expressed despair at the horrible conditions of their imprisonment, let's hope that Sergeant King assured him that the Union would win the war, and then they would be free. If Al was skeptical, Sergeant King could have reminded him that the fall of Vicksburg the previous July had put the whole Mississippi Valley in Northern hands, and that Confederate General Robert E. Lee's push north into Pennsylvania had been turned back at Gettysburg in July as well. If the Confederate government lacked the resources to house and feed its prisoners, where would it find the resources to win the war?

Al thought about this and hoped the older man was right. "We just have to stay alive long enough to see the war's end, Al. So fix your mind on staying alive." Al studied King's auburn hair, bleached now by the relentless sun, and his warm dark eyes, and felt a rush of gratitude for this man beside him. He did his best to keep King sheltered from the relentless sun, for his fair skin burned and puffed up in watery blisters that could so easily become infected and lead to gangrene.

They all talked about what they would do when the war ended, determined they would make it through their present torture. King (a mechanic before the war) and Private Brown (a carpenter) hoped to return to their shops. Most of the others would go back to the family farm. Al, of course, was still a child when he ran away from home and had no idea how he would spend the rest of his life. But listening to this group of older men plan their future gave him a sense that some order must exist in the universe.

At the beginning of April a band of tough bounty jumpers from New York arrived in Andersonville. "They formed themselves into bands numbering from five to twenty-five, each led by a bold,

Bounty jumpers were men who enlisted to receive the bonus or bounty offered, and then went AWOL.

Andersonville Stockade

unscrupulous, energetic scoundrel."[12] These law-breakers began preying on the prisoners, snatching off a blanket or an article of clothing at night. At first they confined their robberies and beatings to the hours of darkness, but soon became so bold that they lifted money and valuables wherever they found them and dominated the camp. If they were caught, their mob of companions came to their rescue.

"Decoys . . . would be on the look-out for promising subjects as each crowd of fresh prisoners entered the gate, and by kindly offers to find them a sleeping place, lure them to where they could be easily disposed of during the night. . . . All men having money or valuables were under continual espionage, and when found in places convenient for attack, . . . they were knocked down and their persons rifled with such swift dexterity that it was done before they realized what had happened."[13] If the victim offered any resistance, the raider would signal for help from other bands. "Severe engagements of this kind were of continual occurrence, in which men were so badly beaten as to die from the effects. The weapons used were fists, clubs, axes, tent-poles, . . . slingshots and brass knuckles. Several of them had succeeded in smuggling bowie-knives into prison."[14]

Al himself wrote that "No one can imagine the terrible slaughter committed each day, the bodies of murdered men were found lying on the ground, some with their pockets turned inside out. Still others had their throats cut. After a while men were murdered in the day time."

If Al asked Sergeant King how the raiders could get away with their thievery, King might have responded, "Well, there's nobody here to prevent them. There are barely enough camp guards to adequately police the exterior of the camp. And the guards haven't any stake in what happens to us. They'd probably be glad if enough of us died that they wouldn't have to deal with the overcrowding and finding food for us."

Al probably protested, "But we don't have any way to protect ourselves or retaliate."

"No, a prison camp is not like the army. We have no officers here to establish discipline and see that basic rules are followed. We have no sheriff or police as you have in regular life, whose duty is to uphold the law. We've reverted to the law of the jungle here—every man for himself."

Al's description continued: "It became so serious that Captain Wirz was notified. He gathered two hundred of us and marched us to the woods and ordered us to cut clubs. We then went back and received orders to organize a committee, elect our chief, who was Peter Aubrey, and a great many others as assistants. He instructed us to arrest the murderers, which made it very exciting for a while." A pitched battle on July 3 broke through the raiders' defenses.

"The work of arresting the leading Raiders went on actively all day on the Fourth of July. They made occasional shows of fierce resistance, but the events of the day before had destroyed their prestige, broken their confidence, and driven away from their support very many who followed their lead when they were considered all-powerful. They scattered from their former haunts and mingled with the crowds in other parts of the prison, but were recognized . . .."[15] The regulators succeeded in arresting 24 of the raider gang. "The Raiders' tents were torn down and pillaged. Blankets, tent poles, and cooking utensils were carried off as spoils, and the ground was dug over for secreted property. A large quantity of watches, chains, knives, rings, gold pens, etc. . . . was found, and helped give impetus to the hunt."[16]

Al wrote that "The murderers were tried and convicted by our own men, and later executed. As they walked upon the scaffold, pillow cases were drawn over their heads and ropes were securely fastened around their necks." On July 11 they were hanged in full sight of all the prisoners. The 18 raiders who were not convicted, when released back into the stockade, were forced to run a gauntlet of prisoners armed with clubs. Three of them died from the beating. Al thought long and hard about this example of frontier justice.

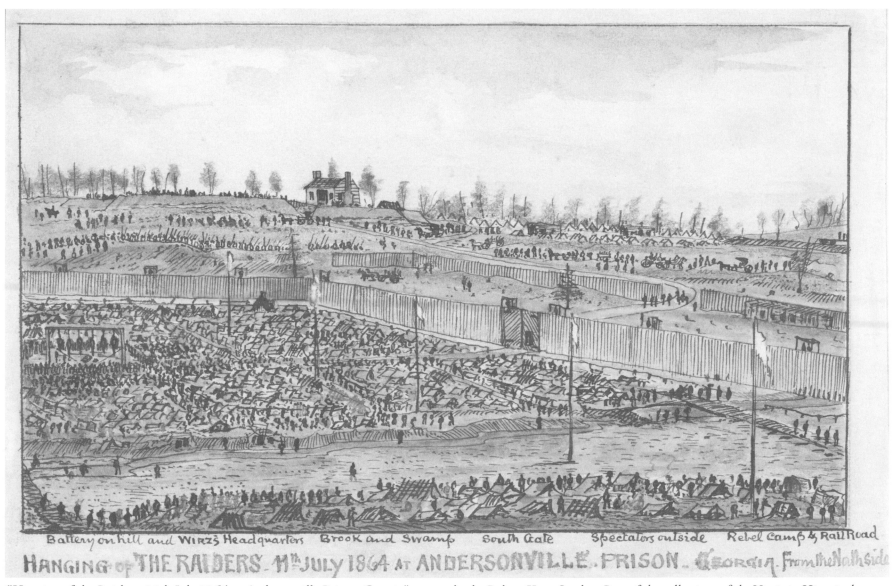

Battery on hill and Wirz's Headquarters   Brook and Swamp   South Gate   Spectators outside   Rebel Camp & Rail Road

HANGING OF THE RAIDERS - 11th JULY 1864 AT ANDERSONVILLE - PRISON - Georgia From the North side

"Hanging of the Raiders, 11th July 1864 at Andersonville Prison, Georgia" watercolor by Robert Knox Sneden. Part of the collections of the Virginia Historical Society.

After the defeat of the bounty jumpers, the prisoners at Andersonville organized themselves and made paths for easier movement. Housing for the Confederate guards is in the foreground, with the stockade behind. Wood engraving by former prisoner Robert Knox Sneden, Library of Congress LC-USZ62-37824.

Al was relieved when, following the executions, a regular police force was recruited from among the prisoners. They were divided into companies, under appropriate officers. Guards were detailed and patrols assigned to oversee the camp, with signals by whistles summoning assistance when needed. These measures gave Al some sense of security.

The low ground inside the stockade deteriorated steadily. Al was used to outhouses. They all were. Those small wooden shacks in every backyard always smelled, even when you spread lime to hurry the disintegration of the excrement. But having to use the swamp in the stockade as a latrine, squatting awkwardly over the rail along its edge, became onerous as the number of men in the stockade increased. Along the stream that ran through the camp the constant milling of men increased the area of the swamp to more than three and a half acres in the middle of the prison. The fecal matter from thousands of men, which bred masses of maggots, became a source of disease for the entire stockade. When spring turned into summer, the stench was unbelievable. Really sick men were too weak to get to the stream, and gradually the smell of urine and excrement pervaded the whole camp.

As the morass along the stream grew, Al and thousands of others went as far up the hill above the swamp as possible to dip drinking water from the stream, but it was already polluted by the Confederate camp outside the stockade. John McElroy wrote that men in his area dug several wells, some as deep as 40 feet. "We had no other tools for this than our ever-faithful half canteens and nothing wherewith to wall the wells. . . . The sides were continually giving away, however, and fellows were perpetually falling down the holes, to the great damage of their legs and arms. The water, which was drawn up in little cans or boot-leg buckets, by strings made of strips of cloth, was much better than that of the creek, but was still far from pure, as it contained seepage from the filthy ground."[17]

In March the prison had held 7,500 men. April saw the number increase to 10,000. In May there were 15,000. During June the number of prisoners within the stockade grew to 29,030 men. In late June, the stockade, originally designed to hold 10,000 men, was enlarged by the addition of 10 acres. By the end of July 31,678 prisoners were inside the stockade, living outdoors, all of them unwashed and wearing filthy, tattered uniforms.

Prisoners at Andersonville. The men in the foreground are using the wooden ledge as a latrine. Photo by A.J. Riddle. Treasures of the Civil War from the New-York Historical Society, Digital ID nhnycw/aa aa02062.

As the weeks went by, Al watched his clothes and his comrades' clothes disintegrate. None of them were well dressed when they arrived, for they had all been through hard campaigning. Now, after weeks digging shelters, scrounging for building materials, cooking over small campfires, sleeping on the sand, and digging wells, they were more tattered and torn than any tramps they had ever seen.

Al wrote in his memoir, "I became assistant cook for the hospital stewards. My garments were terribly worn so that they would not hang together any longer. Then the cook made me a shirt and pants out of cornmeal sacks in the sailor style." Finally Al could discard his blood-soaked shirt.

Al's memoir is as interesting in what it leaves out as in what it tells us. What were his duties as assistant cook? Great cauldrons of cornmeal mush were cooked for the prisoners. Did the prisoners in the hospital receive anything more? Was Al

Andersonville Stockade

confined to the cook house, or did he have contact with those sick enough to be removed from the stockade? Al indicated that as the cook's assistant he was less confined than his companions in the stockade. "I had the privilege of walking a half mile in all directions from the stockade, except south, but was under oath that I would not attempt to escape. I met about thirty other drummer boys in my rambles.

Do a short exercise to visualize this. An acre is about three-quarters of a football field. A football field is 100 yards long (300 feet) and 160 feet wide. The stockade at Andersonville enclosed about 26 acres. Subtract the three-and-a-half-acre swamp in the middle, the stream flowing through, space for various buildings, and a 15-foot "deadline" inside the stockade that served to keep prisoners from charging the walls. That leaves at most 20 acres available for the prisoners. Divide 31,678 men by 20 acres and you find 1,583 men living on a space the size of three-quarters of a football field. How much room did each man have?

"While strolling upon my half-mile limit one day, I noticed two companies of Georgia prison guards encamped not far distant. One of them called to me to come over to where he was. I did so and they asked me all sorts of questions concerning my army. After I replied in regard to the number of soldiers in my army, I was called a liar. The lieutenant took me by the collar and kicked me out and forbade me to talk to them." Why did Al remember this trifling incident, while a description of the hospital is left to John McElroy?

As still more prisoners came in, neither the bread nor the mush was adequate. Those who couldn't be served were issued uncooked rations—a one-half-pound chunk of raw beef and a pound-and-a-half of cornmeal which had been ground up with the husks and cobs, greatly irritating the bowels and causing frightful cramps. Al wrote in his memoir that "we were greatly surprised to find that bread that was baked and was filled with what we supposed was raisins, but after closer inspection we found it to be flies." Al also wrote that "an arm that had been amputated from one of our men on account of gangrene was brought to me by a Confederate surgeon, and he ordered me to cook it until the flesh left the bone. This was a terrible thing to do, but it had to be done."

The men seldom had a plate to receive the food, or wood with which to cook it. A lack of buckets made it difficult to distribute uncooked rice, raw beans, vinegar, or molasses. No salt was available, and the men hungered for it. As autumn approached, prison officials received no more money with which to purchase food.

Andersonville Prison, Georgia, August 17, 1864—southwest view of the stockade showing the deadline, which prisoners were not permitted to cross. Some of the tents are made from sheets sent by the Sanitary Commission of the North in 1864. Civil War photograph collection, Library of Congress LC-US162-122695.

Al watched men pawing through the swamp in the middle of the camp, looking for undigested beans in the excrement, which they ate. He watched men too sick to move die of starvation.

Al wrote that "some were afflicted with moon blindness, which is a very peculiar disease. Running sores appeared below the knees and after sunset the person appeared to be blind, although his eyes were open. During this time another pestilence broke out called scurvy. It usually manifested itself first in the mouth; the gums swelled until they protruded beyond the lips. The teeth became so loose that they frequently fell out, and the sufferer would pick them up and set them back in their sockets. The gums had a fashion of breaking away in large chunks. Scurvy also appeared in the limbs; first the ankle joints swelled, then the foot became useless; then the swelling increased until the knees became stiff. The hands and feet would often drop off, leaving the tendrils projecting out, and the sufferer often dug holes in the ground and remained buried in them up to his waist. Some of the dear boys became so overpowered by the tortures of prison life that they went insane, and this furnished amusement for the Rebels: they practiced shooting and used the poor idiots as targets."

Only the sickest could be hospitalized, and then the doctors had no drugs to treat them, only herbs. "A makeshift of a hospital was established in the northeastern corner of the Stockade. . . . divided from the rest of the prison by a railing, a few tent flies were stretched, and in those the long leaves of the pine were made into apologies for beds . . .. The sick taken there were no better off than if they had staid [sic] with their comrades. . . . Save a few decoctions of roots, there were no medicines; the sick were fed the same coarse corn meal that brought about the malignant dysentery from which they all suffered; they wore and slept in the same vermin-infested clothes . . .."[18] Men died by the hundreds.

Al and Sergeant King watched four of their buddies from the Seventy-fifth Indiana Volunteers die: William A. Lawson of Company A; John N. Wilson of Company G; and Samuel Bock and William Evans of Company I. "Several prayer meetings are held every evening around a small fire, while good men exhort the prisoners, and hymns are sung too, amid the groans and cries of those who are dying all around them."[19]

"It now became a part of the day's regular routine to take a walk past the gates in the morning, inspect and count the dead, and see if any friends were among them. Clothes having by this time become a very important consideration with the prisoners, it was the custom of the mess in which a man died to remove from his person all garments that were of any account, and so many bodies were carried out

John McElroy explained that, hungry as the men were, many of them couldn't eat the half-loaf of cornbread they were given. "Their stomachs revolted against the trash; it became so nauseous to them that they could not force it down, even when famishing, and they died of starvation with the chunks of so-called bread under their head. . . . It was only with the greatest effort—pulling the bread into little pieces and swallowing each of these as one would a pill—that I succeeded in worrying the stuff down."[20]

"We could for a while forget the stench, the lice, the heat, the maggots, the dead and dying around us, the insulting malignancy of our jailors; but it was very hard work to banish thoughts and longings for food from our minds. Hundreds became actually insane from brooding over it. . . . We thought of food all day, and were visited with torturing dreams of it at night. . . . Then I would awake to find myself a half-naked, half-starved, vermin-eaten wretch, crouching in a hole in the ground, waiting for my keepers to fling me a chunk of corn bread."[21]

dead prisoners' names were recorded by Sergeant Dorence Atwater of the Second New York Cavalry.[23] Detailed as a clerk to the surgeon who recorded the daily deaths, Atwater compiled a duplicate list of names and regiments of the deceased, keying them to the numbers inscribed on the posts or boards that were placed over the mass graves. His list of 12,912 names was published after the war, making possible the proper identification of the graves in the huge cemetery at Andersonville.

"One morning [August 13] the camp was astonished beyond measure to discover that during the night a large, bold spring had burst out on the North Side, about midway between the Swamp and the summit of the hill. It poured out its grateful flood of pure, sweet water in an apparently exhaustless quantity. To many who looked in wonder upon it, it seemed as truly a heaven-wrought miracle . . .. The police took charge of the spring, and everyone was compelled to take his regular turn in filling his canteen. This was kept up during our whole stay in Andersonville, and every morning, shortly after daybreak, a thousand men could be seen standing in line, waiting their turns to fill their cans and cups with the precious liquid."[24]

General William Tecumseh Sherman had laid siege to Atlanta in August 1864. The Confederates holding the Georgia city surrendered on September 2. This major setback convinced the prison officials that the prisoners at Andersonville had to be moved. The order came on September 5 to begin moving them all.

"But the Rebel officers lied to us," Al wrote, "telling us we were going to Charleston, South Carolina, to be exchanged. Again we were huddled into freight cars. As we sped on our way, we came to the conclusion that the government we had enlisted to save had forgotten us entirely, and few of us had any hopes of seeing home again. My comrades were dying all around me; my hopes had nearly expired.

John McElroy commented that "it was always the large and strong who first succumbed to hardship. The stalwart, huge-limbed, toil-inured men sank down earliest on the march, yielded soonest to malarial influences, and fell first under the combined effects of home-sickness, exposure and the privations of army life. The slender, withy boys, as supple and weak as cats, had apparently the nine lives of those animals. . . . youths, at the verge of manhood—slender, quick, active, medium-statured fellows, of a cheerful temperament, in whom one would have expected comparatively little powers of endurance."[25] Fortunately Al was one of those slender boys.

Andersonville Stockade

"Nine hundred arrived at Charleston, and at least 80 had died on the way. We were placed in a race-course with no fence around us, and a ploughed furrow answered as the dead line.

"One day a wagon containing clothing and provisions came up from the outside and stopped. A Sister of Mercy alighted and approached the guard and asked permission to distribute it among us, but he refused and ordered her away. Several times she was ordered away, but still she remained. At last she walked to the wagon and grabbed a loaf of bread in each hand and threw it over the guard's head to us. He placed his musket across her bosom and forced her back, but she succeeded in getting away from him and threw more bread to us. Then the guard seized her and placed her in the wagon and drove her away. May God pour his blessings on her noble brow.

"Life was the same here as at Andersonville and we stayed six weeks. Then, boxed up again as beasts, we moved slowly toward Florence, South Carolina. When about 50 miles from Charleston, the train slacked its speed and a poisonous odor filled the air. Looking out, we saw bodies of our men who had jumped for freedom, decaying in the sun. The guard told us that they were shot two weeks before and had layed [*sic*] there ever since to serve as a warning to the rest of us. After gazing on this awful scene of destruction, we resumed our journey. The next morning at daybreak we arrived at Florence.

"I was one in the squad selected by the Rebel guard to gather the dead from the cars. We layed them on the grass a few feet away from the track. Oh what a terrible sight to see those skeleton forms lay mouldering [*sic*] there. Their faces were blue from starvation and the bodies deprived of clothing—76 in all. I watched beside those who were dying and I will never forget it as long as I live."

Between July and November 1864 the Sanitary Commission in the North sent to Andersonville 5,000 sheets, 7,000 pairs of drawers, 4,000 handkerchiefs, 600 overcoats, blankets, shoes, canned milk, coffee, farina (a type of cereal), cornstarch, and tobacco. Private Sneden wrote that all the shoes and much of the clothing was taken by the Rebel officers and guards. [26] The sheets and blankets were immediately made into tents to provide shelter from the hot sun. You can see the difference between drawings of Andersonville made in the spring and photos taken in August.

Al included a verse from a Civil War poem titled "Starved in Prison" by George F. Root (1820-1895):

Had they died in ward or sickroom, nursed with but a soldier's care,

We should grieve, but be thankful that a human heart was there.

Had they fallen in the battle with the old flag waving high,

We should mourn, but not in anguish for the soldiers thus would die.

But the dear boys starved in prison, helpless, friendless and alone,

And their woe can ne'er be spoken nor their agony unknown.

Grounds at Andersonville, Georgia, where 13,000 Union soldiers who died in Andersonville Prison are buried. Includes Clara Barton raising the national flag on August 17, 1865, in background. Wood engraving based on a sketch by J.C. Schotel, Library of Congress LC-DIG-ppmsea-05602.

CHAPTER 9 ENDNOTES

[1] McElroy, p. 71.

[2] McElroy, p. 120.

[3] Found in the National Archives, Record Group 109, "Reports on Conditions at Andersonville Prison," Vol. I, Chapter IX, Vol. 216, 1864-65.

[4] McElroy, p. 120-21.

[5] McElroy, p. 131.

[6] McElroy, p. 153.

[7] Sneden, Private Robert Knox, *Eye of the Storm*, edited by Charles E. Bryan, Jr., and Nelson D. Lankford (New York: Simon & Schuster, 2002), p. 223.

[8] Sneden, p. 249.

[9] McElroy, p. 130.

[10] Sneden, pp. 210-211.

[11] McElroy, p. 164.

[12] McElroy, p. 221.

[13] McElroy, p. 221.

[14] McElroy, p. 222.

[15] McElroy, p. 235.

[16] McElroy, p. 238.

[17] McElroy, p. 208.

[18] McElroy, p. 167.

[19] Sneden, p. 249.

[20] McElroy, p. 340.

[21] McElroy, pp. 340-41.

[22] McElroy, p. 154.

[23] Information about Atwater comes from the National Park Civil War Series, text by William G. Burnett, *The Prison Camp at Andersonville* (Eastern National Park and Monument Association, 1995).

[24] McElroy, p. 353.

[25] McElroy, p. 165.

[26] Sneden, p. 252.

Union prisoners being counted by guards at Florence Stockade. Florence military prison series of watercolors by James E. Taylor, Library of Congress LC-USZ62-121343.

Florence Stockade

Chapter 10   Florence Stockade

Al's memoir continues: "My bunkmates Fogarty and Johnson assisted me in giving them water as that was all we had to give. We tried rubbing their arms to restore their circulation, but to no effect. They were nearer the next world than this. We marched up to the stockade, which seemed exactly like that of Andersonville, but not quite as large. The Lieutenant promised Fogarty that he would try and get us the position of gravediggers. We remained inside the stockade about two weeks when one day the Lieutenant came to us and said he had seen Colonel John Iverson, who commanded at Florence, and that the Colonel had directed him to take us to him. When we reached Iverson's quarters, which was an old log house, he administered our parole oath. There was about 28 of us, and Fogarty was chosen sergeant of our squad. We were now no longer under guards, for we were on parole. We went two miles to a heavy pine forest. Axes and good rations were given to us, and Lieutenant Reese told us to work and build a house.

"Indeed we did, and happiness reigned supreme. We built three log huts and had plenty to eat. Also cooking utensils, straw, and blankets. Johnson wept with joy. The future seemed brighter again, and we were inspired with greater expectations and patriotism.

"Lieutenant Reese led the way to where the new graveyard was to be, and early the next morning we commenced our work. A trench was dug 60 feet long, six and one-half feet wide, and only two and one-half feet deep, as it was impossible to dig deeper on account of the hard red clay beneath. Three wagon loads of dead bodies were piled up. There were 44 in all, ready to be layed [sic] away in their everlasting resting place. It seemed hard to lay the poor weak skeletons down in the cold ground without even a shroud, and yet it seemed better than to see them starving and dying by inches.

Drummer Boy of Company C

Prisoners who have left Florence Stockade, being greeted by Union soldiers. Note the boxcars and steam engine of the train. Florence military prison series of watercolors by James E. Taylor, Library of Congress LC-USZ62-117628.

122

sight of Port Royal and saw the glorious old flag floating in the air over our ships that lay at anchor. Several of the boys who were unable to rise asked us to lift them up so that they might see the stars and stripes once more. Arriving up along the steamers that were anchored, planks were laid down from one to the other, and there stood two old gray-haired surgeons ready to assist us aboard.

"How the tears trickled down their cheeks as they carefully helped the poor weak skeletons aboard and gave us a cup of coffee and a cracker, with the promise of more. We then moved to the next ship and were ordered to take off our prison rags and were given shower baths and new blue suits. Then we marched to the next ship, which was to carry us home.

"I cannot describe the happiness at the thought of seeing home again once more. Some laughed and sang, others prayed."

CHAPTER 10 ENDNOTES

[1] McElroy, p. 544.
[2] McElroy, p. 548.
[3] McElroy, p. 558.

Prisoners embarked by boat from South Carolina for their trip to Maryland because some of the railroads were still in Confederate hands. "Embarkation of exchanged Union prisoners at Aiken's Landing, February 21, 1865," shows prisoners boarding the steamboat New York. *Illustration by J.R. Hamilton published in* Harper's Weekly *March 18, 1865, Library of Congress LC-USZ62-132751.*

Free at last

CHAPTER 11   Free at last

An exchange of 5,000 prisoners was arranged late in 1864.[1] The prisoners were sent through Confederate lines at Port Royal, South Carolina. The exchange was made at Venus Landing in November 1864. Al wrote in his memoir that "after reaching Fortress Monroe [at the entrance to the Chesapeake Bay], we sailed up the Chesapeake to Annapolis, Maryland, and here we were placed in a parole camp." On December 5, Al was sent by ship to College Green Barracks, Maryland. On December 10, 1864, he was moved on to Camp Parole, Maryland. He was furloughed to go to Camp Chase, Ohio, where he reported on January 16, 1865. Camp Chase had been a training camp for Northern soldiers and a parole camp for Confederate prisoners. It finally became a mustering-out facility for Union soldiers.

Nothing in the records indicates what shape Al was in after more than a year as a prisoner of war. He had been fortunate at both Andersonville and Florence to be taken out of the mass of prisoners and given something to do. Certainly he was thin, for in the final months at Andersonville and Florence there had been very little to eat. The food was better after his exchange. There is no indication that he suffered from the chronic diarrhea, dysentery, and scurvy that felled so many prisoners of war, other than the fact that he developed asthma years later and applied for a pension.

Finally having a bath. Florence military prison series of watercolors by James E. Taylor, Library of Congress LC-USZ62-126376.

had shared hardship and fear and danger and had looked after one other. They had come to hate war and the army and were passionately eager to take off their uniforms and go home. But would they ever again share that kind of bond? They all had lumps in their throats without being able to articulate the emotions they shared. The men around him were his comrades, and intuition told him that kind of comradeship might be a rare thing.

The Seventy-fifth Indiana Infantry Volunteers was formally mustered out at Washington on June 8, 1865. They boarded a train to Parkersburg, West Virginia, then a steamer down the Ohio River. Another train took them to Indianapolis, where they marched to the arsenal and turned it their guns and equipment. The governor gave a public reception at the Capitol. The troops stayed at Camp Morton until June 16, when their discharges were handed to them.[3]

Al's memoir, however, ends in the North Carolina woods. There is no mention of the victory parade in Washington or the journey home. What he remembered years later was his comrades' suffering. His final words were "I cannot help but feel sorrowful when my memory goes back to the past, and I recall how some of the boys prayed to die and others prayed to live. Had they died on the field of battle, we would have felt differently, but they died by inches in the most miserable of places and with the most miserable treatment."

Four years earlier Al had left home, embarking on what he thought would be a grand adventure. He had participated in a major military campaign, survived the fierce battle at Chickamauga, and spent 14 months as a POW. He had traveled around a large section of the southeastern United States. On May 24 he had marched down Pennsylvania Avenue in the nation's capital—Jacob carrying the Stars and Stripes, Al beating his new drum: the Grand Army of the Republic, victorious.

Facing page: Grand Review of the Armies, a military celebration in Washington, D.C., on May 23, 1865. Major General George Gordon Meade led the 80,000 men of the Army of the Potomac from Capitol Hill down Pennsylvania Avenue. The infantry marched 12 men abreast across the road, followed by the divisional and corps artillery, then an array of cavalry regiments that stretched for seven miles. On the reviewing stand in front of the White House were President Johnson, General-in-Chief Ulysses S. Grant, senior military leaders, the Cabinet, and leading government officials. On the following day General William Tecumseh Sherman led the 65,000 men of the Armies of Tennessee, Georgia, and Ohio on a six-hour review. Civil War-Era Photographs, National Archives 111-BA-69.

Free at last

Drummer Boy of Company C

Compared to the raw boy who had run away almost four years earlier, Al felt now like a war-weary veteran. He was 18 years old, a man proven in adversity, and now he was going home.

Tramp, tramp, tramp, the boys are marching,
Cheer up, comrades, they will come.
And beneath the starry flag, we shall breathe the air again
Of the free land and our own beloved home.

Chapter 11 Endnotes

[1] Al's name appears in the "Records of Exchanged Federal Prisoners of War of the Untied States Army released at Baton Rouge, La., Galveston, Texas, Charleston, S.C., and Savannah, Ga., from Nov. 18, '64 to Dec. 31, '64, Vol. 8, Part 3, R to Z. Prepared in the Office of the Commissary General of Prisoners from rolls filed in his office," National Archives Record Group 249, Entry 72. Al also appears in the "Records of Paroled Federal Prisoners of War of the United States Army, received and sent from Camp Parole Annapolis, Md., from Nov. 17th 1864 to June 19th 1865, Vol. 4 Part 9, W to Z. Prepared in the Office of the Commissary General of Prisoners from rolls filed in his Office," National Archives Record Group 249, Entry 69.

[2] This information comes from an affidavit Al wrote in Lair's behalf in 1902. The full text of the affidavit appears in the Afterword.

[3] Al's discharge papers are in National Archives Record Group 94, Office of the Adjutant General, Enlisted Branch, Box No. 2346.

Free at last

AFTERWORD

Where did Al's mother Emily and his sister Josephine and his half-brother Robert spend the war? And how did they survive with no man to provide for them? Did Al send his mother his monthly pay, $12 a month when he was mustered in (a dollar less than a private received), increased in 1865 to $16 a month? That doesn't sound like much, but the average annual family income in the United States in 1860 was about $600, or $50 a month. Many families lived on much less than $50 a month, and $16 would have been an important sum. How did his mother manage in the year Al was imprisoned and received no pay? She would have been very happy when he received his back pay for the months he spent in prison.

Information on Al's salary comes from a certificate of payment included in his Compiled Military Service Record, National Archives.

Al's life after the war can be gleaned from a variety of documents. On May 16, 1869, he married Mary J. Hughes of Marion County, Indiana.[1] My father remembered that they had a daughter named Mabel, who must have been born after 1870 because she did not appear in the 1870 census. In the 1870 census Almon was listed in Marion County, Indiana, as a cigar manufacturer. His wife "keeps house." His mother Emily was living with them, as was her 15-year-old son Emerce.[2] Three other people were listed at the same address. Perhaps they were boarders.

My father said that his father Almon was never robust enough to do heavy physical work. Making cigars would have taken manual dexterity rather than strength. The 1873 Indianapolis City Directory listed Almon Beneway as a cigar maker living at 43 Hosbrook. In 1874 he was listed as a cigar maker living at 172 Eddy, along with his mother Mrs. Emily Beneway. In 1876 Almon and his half-brother Robert were both listed as cigar makers, both located at 453 East Market (possibly a business address), while Al's wife Mary was listed at 47 Hosbrook.

As long as he lived in Indianapolis, Al probably went to reunions of the Grand Army of the Republic, where he sat with his old buddies as they refought the battles they had waged together and told David Bittle Floyd, the regimental historian, what they remembered of the war. Let's hope he was reunited with Sergeant King at some of the reunions. If that happened, Al would have been overjoyed to see his old mentor and friend on his feet, although his joints were knotted and bent. Rheumatism had been added to his burdens, making him eligible for a military pension as early as 1869. Still, King lived for 30 more years, dying in Soldier's Home in Dayton, Ohio, in 1902.

Al's wife Mary and his daughter Mabel both died in the 1870s, and in 1876 Al moved back to Dutchess County in New York State on the lower Hudson River, where he was born. The 1877-80 Poughkeepsie City Directories listed A. B. Beneway, cigar manufacturer; Emily Beneway, widow; and Robert Beneway, cigar maker.

In the 1880 census Almon was living in Poughkeepsie, along with his half-brother and his sister Josephine. The death records for that year include Emily Beneway, Almon's mother. Al married Ardelle Wooden in 1881.

The 1876-82 Poughkeepsie City Directories list Josephine Lair. This was the first indication that Josephine had married Al's buddy and led me to seek further information on Jacob Lair.

According to the 1860 census, Jacob was born in Nebraska and lived there with his parents and several siblings. Jacob and Josephine Lair were listed in the 1870 census living in Indianapolis. Jacob was a cooper. In 1876 Jacob was listed as residing alone in Atchison County, Missouri, presumably homesteading. Did Josephine insist that he have a house for her to live in before she would join him? In 1880 Jacob was listed, alone, in St. Louis, Missouri.

In June 1890 Jacob Lair was listed on a "Special Schedule of Surviving Soldiers, Sailors, and Marines, and Widows, etc. Residing in Fulton Township,

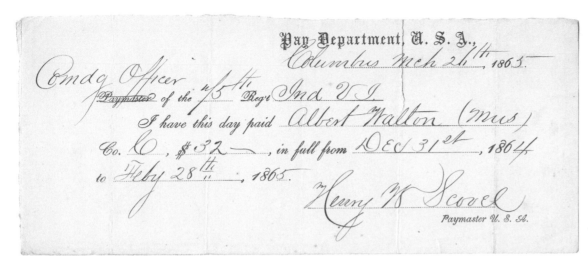

Certificate of payment dated March 25, 1865, indicating that the paymaster paid Albert Walton $32 for service in January and February of 1865. Compiled Military Service Record, National Archives.

Callaway County, Missouri." In 1894 Jacob was granted a homestead of 160 acres of land in Missouri.

Further research led me to Jacob Lair's pension file, which revealed that he married Josephine Lair on July 20, 1865. He apparently did not go back to his family in Nebraska. Al must have taken Jacob home with him when they were mustered out in June. Jacob and Josephine married a month later.

Al's statement on an affidavit in Jacob's pension file reads as follows: "I know Jacob Lair as duty Sergent [sic] and color bearer. Still later as first Lieut. of the Company C, 75 Ind, which I was a member of during the Civil War. I remember his suffering in the march and camp by reason I was his bunkmate. Yet still he was allways [sic] with us from the start to the finish, that is from '62 to '65. I cannot remember a more gallant or braver soldier in our Co than him. He was always at his Post of Duty."

In Jacob's pension file are two affidavits written by "Albert Walton" Beneway, the first on September 3, 1901: "These facts are personnally [sic] known to me by reason I was with the command at the time that he was treated for fever. I was his bunkmate. I turned him over when he was so low, from side to side. I as many others of his comrades did not think he would live. This was while we were encamped at Frankfort, KY, in 1862. I have known him 38 years. I have also saw his distress and sufferings for years since that war from chronic dourah [sic] and rheumatism and I well remember his suffering while on the march. Yet he was always at his Post, but how he kept there is a mystery yet to this day to me."

The second affidavit was filed on January 8, 1902. Al filled out a form stating that "We returned home together and lived together until 1876 July when I came to NY where I have since lived. He [Jacob] suffered from Acholic [sic] diarrhea. At times he was in great pain and frequent running off of the bowels. I saw him constantly and daily. He was disabled about one fourth of the year. I last saw him July 1876. Have not seen him since, but hear from him often as he writes to me and described [sic] to me his sufferings by mail."[3]

3–373.
(Old No. 3–056.)

WESTERN Div.   , Ex'r.

Inv. Cy. No. 661054

Jacob Lair
Co. 75 2nd Iny.
Act of July 14, 1902

Department of the Interior,
BUREAU OF PENSIONS,

Washington, D. C., Jan 8, 1902

Sir:—

To further aid this Bureau in determining the merits of the above-entitled claim for pension, be kind enough to answer in your own handwriting the following questions, giving more complete details than your affidavit affords.

Very respectfully,

Mr Albert Walton Beneway.
Clinton Hollow
New York.

N. Clay Evans
Commissioner.

When did you first see the soldier after he returned from the army, and how do you fix the date? at Indianapolis Ind

Answer: We returned home together and lived together until 1876 July When I came to NY Where I have Since lived (1865)

Of what disability did he then complain, and how was he affected?

Answer: Chronic dihhea at times he was In great Pain and frequent running off of the bowells

Did he continue to suffer from said disability? If so, please state how frequently you saw him, what symptoms you observed, and the extent to which he was disabled for the performance of manual labor during each year.

Answer: I saw him Constantly and daily he was disabled about one fourth of the year I last Saw him July 1876 have not Saw him Since but hear from him often as he writes to me and discribes to me his Sufferings by mail

Very respectfully,
Albert Walton Beneway

The COMMISSIONER OF PENSIONS.

NOTE.—If the witness is unable to write, it is suggested that he request some competent person to aid him in replying to this circular; his mark to be attested by the postmaster or some other United States official, who should certify that the contents of the paper were fully made known to the witness before his mark was placed thereon.

0–4

Adjutant General's Office,
Washington, D. C.,
May 24, 18—.

Sir:

I have the honor to acknowledge the receipt from your Office of application for Pension No. 1420048, and to return it herewith, with such information as is furnished by the files of this Office.

It appears from the Rolls on file in this Office, that Wesley King was enrolled on the 14th day of July, 1862, at Tipton in Co. B, 75 Regiment of Indiana Volunteers, to serve three years, or during the war, and mustered into service as a Sergeant on the 19th day of August 1862, at Indianapolis, in Co. B, 75 Regiment of Indiana Volunteers, to serve three years, or during the war. On the Muster Rolls of Co. B of that Regiment, for the months from enrollment to Aug 31st 1863, he is reported "Present", Roll for Sept and Oct 1863 reports him "Missing in Action at Chickamauga Sept 20th 1863, Roll for Nov & Apl 1864 reports him "Wounded at Chickamauga Ga and captured by the Enemy, Sept 20th 1863". He is reported on Rolls of Co. absent from Sept 20th 1863 to March 1st 1865. On Roll for March + April 1865 he appears "Present". On M O Roll dated June 8th 1865 he is mustered out and discharged with Co. H.D. with remark "Exchanged Prisoner."

B
H.D.

Records Prisoners of War show that Wesley King, Sgt. Co. "B", 75th Indiana Vols, was captured at Chickamauga, — Sept. 20, 1863, delivered on parole at Charleston, S. C. Dec. 13, 1864, reported at Camp Parole, Md. (date not stated,) furloughed Dec. 26, 1864 for 30 days to report to Camp Chase, Ohio, reported at Camp Chase, Jany 26, 1865, furloughed for 20 days, and was sent to Provost Marshal April 1, 1865. No further information.

Above: Albert "Walton" Beneway's affidavit in Jacob Lair's pension file, National Archives. Right: A form from Wesley King's pension file indicating his years of service. National Archives.

In the 1890 census Jacob Lair was listed alone, living in Nebraska. In the 1900 census, Josephine was again listed with her husband Jacob, living in Callaway County, Missouri. In the 1910 census Jacob was listed alone, living in Fulton Township, Missouri. In a form Jacob filled out for the Bureau of Pensions in 1915 he indicated that his wife was dead. In the 1920 census Jacob lived alone in Hempstead County, Arkansas. This limited sketch of his life may indicate that Jacob, having experienced much hand-to-hand combat during the war, had difficulty adjusting to civilian life, as happens with many of our soldiers today.

Returning to Almon: the 1900 census listed Almon as a farmer, age 53, living in Clinton Town in Dutchess County, along with his wife Ardelle, age 39; his half-brother Robert E. Beneway; and his children, John, Frank, Raymond, Della, Almon, Ernest, Chester, and Myrtle. Almon gave his son Ernest the middle name "Lair."

My father remembered that as the children came along the parents decided that they did not want to raise them in the city. In 1882 they moved out to a small farm in Shultzville (where Almon's second wife Ardelle had been born), 20 miles north of Poughkeepsie. Almon could no longer compete with machine-made cigars, so he kept a small store and post office in Shultzville, while his half-brother Robert and his sons did the farm work.

"Alb't Walton Beneway" was listed in the Dutchess County pension rolls of 1885 as having received a pension of $10 monthly since 1881 because of asthma.

In 1901 the farmhouse burned down, destroying all of their furniture. The family then moved to a small farm at Clinton Hollow, four miles to the south. Son John had died. Both my father and his brother Almon Jr. found jobs. The farm didn't support the family, so in 1908 they moved to Poughkeepsie. My father and his brother Al bought a house for their parents. In the 1910 census my grandfather Almon was listed with no occupation and had another daughter, Grace.

Almon died in 1926, the year that I was born. Throughout my life he has been a heroic, rather mythical figure who was captured at Chickamauga and suffered

Almon, a second lieutenant in Company A of the Twenty-first Regiment, New York State Militia. The date of the photo is unknown, but my guess is around 1900, when Almon would have been participating in a state militia activity. After 1906 he belonged to the New York National Guard, formally organized that year.

His wife Ardelle. Author's collection.

Afterword

through Andersonville. Now that I have retraced his steps and put flesh on his bones, I see him as an eager, somewhat reckless youngster who craved adventure. Little did he know how he would come of age in the crucible of the Civil War.

ENDNOTES FOR AFTERWORD

[1] Indiana Marriage Collection, 1800-1941, found on <www.ancestry.com>.
[2] In the 1860 census Emily's son was named Emile.
[3] Jacob Lair's pension file, National Archives.

ALMON BENEWAY'S WAR RECORD FULL WITH ADVENTURES

Death of 79-Year Old Veteran Recalls His Fine Services For Union

WAS DRUMMER BOY

Enlisted at 14 Despite Two Previous Futile Attempts —Prisoner, Too

The funeral of Almon Beneway, 79, Saturday, recalled to veterans of the Civil War his stirring experiences in the war as a drummer boy. A regimental history discloses that at fourteen after two unsuccessful attempts to become a drummer boy, Mr. Beneway came to Louisville. Previously he had been refused admission to the 19th Indians at Camp Morton, Indianapolis, but followed them for three months in Virginia. He was taken sick with typhoid fever and sent to a Washington hospital. Still lacking the consent of his mother, he returned to Indianapolis and was refused admission to the 16th Indians.

When the 15th Indians left Indianapolis Almon Beneway followed it as a cymbal player. In Kentucky nea Mumfordsville most of the regiment was captured. The boy escaped with others and returned to Louisville. Finally the boy's application was accepted, although the company he entered had no musician. Captain Bryant ordered the purchase of a drum and so on September 1, 1862, Almon O. Beneway was mustered into the service under the name of Albert Walton, a blue-eyed, brown haired and beardless boy. He was the musician of C Company of the 75th Regiment at the age of 15. He was four feet seven inches tall, the smallest member of the regiment.

He was badly wounded in field hospital work at Cloud's. For fourteen months he was held prisoner at Richmond and Danville in Virginia, at Andersonville in Georgia and at Charleston and Florence in South Carolina. On November 30, 1864, he was paroled and returned to the federal lines.

When "Al," as the boy was known, helped James E. Kidden of C Company from the field of Chickamauga, wounded, the right side of the drummer's blouse was so saturated it was as stiff as a board. There was no opportunity to wash it and he wore it in that condition during his long imprisonment.

Funeral services were held yesterday afternoon from his late home at 4 Virginia avenue at 1:30 o'clock, the Rev. Alexander B. MacLeod officiating. Burial was at Schultzville.

Mr. Beneway was 79 years old, having been born in Oneida County in 1847. His boyhood was spent in Indianapolis. After the war his family moved to Poughkeepsie, where he received a commission as second lieutenant in the 21st Regiment. He served as postmaster at Schultzville during the administration of President McKinley.

ALMON BENEWAY DIES AT HOME

Veteran's Funeral Will Take Place Saturday

Almon Beneway, 79, Civil War veteran, died at his home, 4 Virginia avenue, yesterday afternoon after a long period of ill health. Services will be held Saturday afternoon at 1:30 o'clock, from the residence, with the Rev. Alexander C. Mac-

ALMON B. BENEWAY

Leod, pastor of the Congregational church officiating. Burial will be in Schultzville under the direction of Frank K. Dean.

Mr. Beneway was born in Oneida county in 1847. His parents moved to Indianapolis, Ind., shortly after, where he spent his boyhood. At the age of 14, he enlisted in the Indiana Volunteers as a drummer boy, and served four years in the Civil War.

Toward the close of the war, he was captured by the Confederates and confined in the Andersonville prison, where he stayed until the signing of peace. After the war, his family moved to Poughkeepsie where he joined Company A of the old 21st Regiment, receiving a second lieutenant's commission. Mr. Beneway entered the cigar manufacturing field in 1882, moving to Schultzville, where he kept a store and served as postmaster during the administration of President McKinley, in addition to his cigar-making. Some years later the family returned to this city.

He is survived by his wife, Mrs. Ardelle Beneway, six sons, John E. of Roxbury, Mass.; Frank W., of Ontario; Raymond, Almon W., Ernest L, and Chester H., all of this city, and three daughters, Mrs. Myrtle Savino, Mrs. Grace Flores and Mrs. Ardell Constable.

Hamilton Sleight Post, G. A. R., Colonel Harry Murray commanding, will hold military services in conjunction with the religious rites at the home.

Almon's obituary says that he was born in Oneida County, New York. Newspapers are secondary sources, and often make mistakes. Almon was born in Clinton Town (or Clinton Hollow) in Dutchess County, near Poughkeepsie. The newspaper editor saw "Clinton" and assumed it meant the more populous Clinton, New York, which is in Oneida County.

Obituary of Almon Beneway from the Poughkeepsie Enterprise, *April 1926.*

PRIMARY SOURCES

Almon's Memoir: a 24-page, hand-written, unpublished document, dictated in about 1920.

Harper's Weekly (A Journal of Civilization), an American political magazine based in New York. Published by Harper & Brothers from 1857 until 1916, it featured foreign and domestic news, fiction, essays on many subjects, and humor, along with many illustrations.

House of Representatives, 37th Congress, 2d Session, Ex. Doc. No. 79, "Regimental Bands," Letter from the Secretary of War, 1862.

House of Representatives, 38th Congress, 2d Session, Ex. Doc. No. 2, Letters from the Secretary of the Treasury, "Estimates of Additional Appropriations, 1865" and Ex. Doc. No. 83, *Annual Report of the Secretary of War, 1865.*

John McElroy, *Andersonville, a Story of Rebel Military Prisons, Fifteen months a Guest of the So-called Southern Confederacy* (Toledo, Ohio: D.R. Locke, 1879).

Library of Congress, Prints and Photographs Division Digital Collections <www.loc.gov/pictures>:

> *Andersonville Prison Photographs*
> *Civil War Photographs*
> *Morgan Collection of Civil War Drawings*
> *Photographs of the War of the Rebellion*

National Archives Textual Records (Washington, D.C.):

Record Group 15, Records of the Department of Veterans Affairs, 1773 - 2007

Military Pension Records (of Seventy-fifth Indiana Volunteer soldiers wounded or captured at Chickamauga):

Sergeant Jacob Lair	Private John N. Wilson
Sergeant Wesley King	Private Byron Kurtz
Private William H. Bortsfield	Private Edmund H. Brown
Sergeant John Rhine	Private Samuel Bock
Private Jeremiah Sherman	First Lieutenant William McGinnis
Private William A. Lawson	

Record Group 94, Records of the Adjutant General's Office, 1762 - 1984

Compiled Military Service Records (of Seventy-fifth Indiana Volunteer soldiers wounded or captured at Chickamauga):

Musician Albert Walton
Sergeant Jacob Lair
Surgeon Christopher S. Arthur
Assistant Surgeon Abner H. Shaffer
Private James E. Kidder
Sergeant Wesley King
First Lieutenant William McGinnis
Corporal Hayden H. Rayborn
Private David M. Cox
Private James R. Quinn
Private Samuel B. Weaver
Private John B. Whistler
Private Edmund H. Brown
Private John D. McKee
Private Byron Kurtz
Private William Evans
Private Samuel Bock
Private John Wilson
Private James M. Lawson
Private William A. Lawson
Private Jeremiah Sherman
Private John Rhine

Private Daniel Wilcoxon
Private Samuel Sanders
Private Christopher Bowlin
Private John Calvin Patton
Private Henry Snyder
Private James Thorington
Private David F. Johnson
Private John C. Malsby
Private Edmund H. Brown
Private Joseph I. Johnson
Private George Nevins
Private George F. Smith
Private Lewis R. Fitch
Private Calvin Burcham
Private John Elzie
Private John McGrath
Private Loren G. King
Private James Dearinger
Private Sylas Moorehead
Private Isaac H. Watson
Private William H. Bortsfield

Entry 409 (PI-17), Enlisted Branch Files, 1862 - ca. 1890. Box No. 2346 contains discharge papers of Almon Beneway.

Entries 112 - 115 (PI-17), Regimental and Company Books of Civil War Volunteer Union Organizations, 1861 - 1865

Microfilm No. M594, Compiled Records Showing Service of Military Units in Volunteer Union Organizations, Indiana Rolls 38, 44, and 45

Record Group 109, War Department Collection of Confederate Records, 1825 - 1927

Confederate Record Books Relating to Prisoners and Prisons, 1861 - 1865, "Report on Conditions at Andersonville Prison," Vol. 1, Chapter IX, Vol. 216, 1864-65: Joseph Jones, Surgeon, P. & C.S., Professor of Medicine (Chemistry) in the Medical College of Georgia, at Augusta, Ga.: "Observations upon the Disease of the Federal Prisoners confined in Camp Sumpter Andersonville, in Sumpter County, Georgia, instituted with a view to illustrate chiefly the Origins & Causes of Hospital Gangrene, the Relations of Continued & Malarial Fevers, and the Pathology of Camp Diarrhoea & Dysentery" (hand written)

Record Group 249, Records of the Commissary General of Prisoners

Entry 69 (NM-68), Vol. 19 of 28, Records of the Commissary General of Prisoners, Paroled Prisoners of War, "Registers of arrivals and departures of Paroled Federal prisoners of war at Camp Parole, MD, 1862-1865"

Entry 72 (NM-68), Vol. 25 of 33, Records of the Commissary General of Prisoners, "Registers of Exchanged Federal Prisoners of War, 1861-1865"

Entry 142 (NM-68), Records of the Commissary General of Prisoners, Prisoner of War Division of the Adjutant General's Office, 1861-1905, Name Index to Series 26, 31, 35, 42, 53-55, 62, 106, 109, "Miscellaneous Records of Prisoners of War"

National Archives Photographs (College Park, Maryland):

Record Group 111: Records of the Office of the Chief Signal Officer, 1860-1985

Entry 111-B "Mathew Brady Photographs of Civil War-Era Personalities and Scenes, compiled 1921-1940, documenting the period 1860-1865"

Entry 111-BA "Civil War-Era Photographs, compiled ca. 1921"

Record Group 165: Records of the War Department and Special Staffs, 1860-1952

Entry 165-S, "Military Fortifications and National Cemeteries, compiled 1865-1866"

Entry 165-SB, "'Photographic Sketchbook of the Civil War,' by Alexander Gardner, compiled ca. 1861 - ca. 1865"

New-York Historical Society, *Treasures of the Civil War Collection*, New York, New York

Patrick, Jeffrey L., and Robert J. Willey, editors, *Fighting for Liberty and the Right: The Civil War Diary of William Bluffton Miller* (Knoxville, Tennessee: University of Tennessee Press, 2005)

"Personal Recollections of Chickamauga" in *Sketches of War History, 1861-1865: Papers Read before the Ohio Commandery of the Military Order of the Loyal Legion of the United States, 1883-1886,* Vol. I (Wilmington, North Carolina: Broadfoot, 1991, reprint of 1888 edition)

Scott, Harold L., Sr., editor, *The Civil War Memoirs of Little Red Cap: A drummer boy at Andersonville Prison* (Cumberland, Maryland, 1997)

United States Army Regulations of 1861 with an Appendix containing the Changes and Laws Affecting Army Regulations and Articles of War to June 25, 1863. Found at <http://quod.lib.umich.edu>

Werner, Emmy E., *Reluctant Witnesses: Children's Voices from the Civil War* (Boulder, Colorado: Westview Press, 1998)

SECONDARY SOURCES

Battles and Leaders of the Civil War, Volume III, V (New York: The Century Company, 1884)

Catton, Bruce, *This Hallowed Ground* (Garden City, New York: Doubleday & Co., Inc., 1956)

Burnett, William G., T*he Prison Camp at Andersonville*, National Park Civil War Series (Eastern National Park and Monument Association, 1995)

Floyd, David Bittle, *History of the Seventy-fifth Regiment of Indiana Infantry Volunteers* (Philadelphia: Lutheran Publication Society, 1893)

Haislip, Phyllis Hall, *Marching in Time: The Colonial Williamsburg Fife and Drum Corps* (Richmond, Virginia: the Dietz Press, 2003)

Kieffer, Henry Mertyn, *The Recollections of a Drummer Boy* (Boston: Ticknor and Company, 1889). Reproduced by the Library of Congress, 2010

Lord, Francis A. and Arthur Wise, *Bands and Drummer Boys of the Civil War* (South Brunswick, New Jersey: Thomas Yoseloff Ltd., 1966)

Sanders, Charles W., *While in the Hands of the Enemy* (Baton Rouge: Louisiana State University Press, 2005)

Sneden, Private Robert Knox, *Eye of the Storm*, edited by Charles F. Bryan, Jr., and Nelson D. Lankford (New York: Simon & Schuster, 2000)

Sneden, Private Robert Knox, *Images from the Storm*, edited by Charles F. Bryant, Jr., James C. Kelly, and Nelson D. Lankford (New York: The Free Press, 2001)

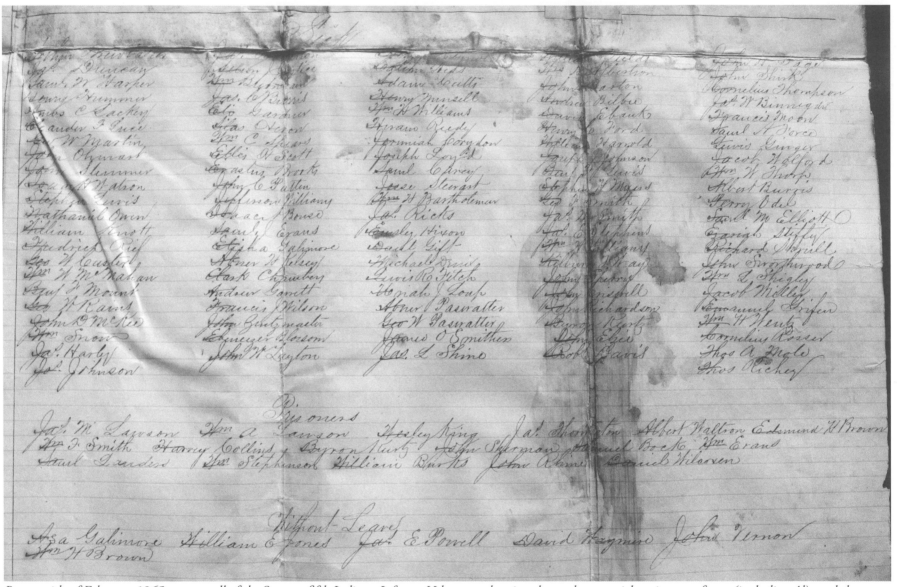

Reverse side of February 1865 muster roll of the Seventy-fifth Indiana Infantry Volunteers showing those who were sick, prisoners of war (including Al), and those who were AWOL. National Archives Record Group 94.

Sources

Index

ABOUT THE AUTHOR

Author Mary Louise Clifford with her daughter Candace, a maritime historian, who assisted with researching Al in the National Archives and finding the illustrations. The Cliffords have collaborated on five lighthouse titles including Women Who Kept the Lights: An Illustrated History of Female Lighthouse Keepers, *which will appear in 2013 in a 20th anniversary third edition. Both live in Alexandria, Virginia.*

Mary Louise Clifford is the author of twenty-some books, ranging in subject from Afghanistan to lighthouse keepers. For over 50 years she has been collecting information about her grandfather, the drummer boy of Company C in the Seventy-fifth Indiana Infantry Volunteer Regiment. She takes great satisfaction in finally presenting here the story of his Civil War experiences.

For information on her other books, visit her website at www.MaryLouiseClifford.com.